# MY ANCESTORS WERE BAPTISTS

## HOW CAN I FIND OUT MORE ABOUT THEM?

by
Geoffrey R Breed

SOCIETY OF GENEALOGISTS 2002

Published by
**Society of Genealogists Enterprises Ltd**
14 Charterhouse Buildings
Goswell Road
London EC1M 7BA


First Published 1986
Revised 1988
Third Edition 1995
Fourth Edition 2002

British Library Cataloguing
in Publication Data.
A catalogue record for this book is
available from the British Library


ISBN 1 903462 52 5


Society of Genealogists Enterprises Limited is a wholly owned subsidiary
of Society of Genealogists, a registered charity, no 233701.
Company Number 3899591  VAT Number 749 5602103

The Reverend Geoffrey Ralph Breed was educated at the City of London School and
Edinburgh University, where he read Science. After service as an Army Officer he had
a successful career in commerce, later studying Theology at Christ Church College,
Canterbury and entering the Baptist ministry. A Baptist historian, his postgraduate
studies included an M.A. in history at Keele University.

The cover illustration is from the first Minute of Stroud Baptist Church,
Gloucestershire, and is reproduced by kind permission of the Church.

# CONTENTS

# LIST OF ILLUSTRATIONS

# PREFACE TO THE FOURTH EDITION

Whereas the text has been up-dated and slightly enlarged, Appendix 2 has been entirely re-written. In previous editions the list of registers at the Public Record Office (Class RG 4) has been extracted from the 1859 publication of HM Stationery Office, *Lists of Non-Parochial Registers and Records in the Custody of the Registrar-General of Births, Deaths and Marriages*, and the PRO references added in. In that publication the span of years covered by each register had been calculated from the dates of the first and last entries contained in it. A continuing project by the PRO to examine every single register, to ascertain the actual starting and finishing dates of each, has now been completed, and this corrected information has been included in this Fourth Edition. Some registers which were not surrendered to the State in the late 1830s, as required, have subsequently been deposited with the PRO, who have classed them as 'RG 8 - Unauthenticated Registers'. These, too, have all been included in this current listing.

The registers held in Class RG 4 at the Public Record Office are included in the International Genealogical Index (IGI) compiled by the Genealogical Society of Utah. They are arranged by English counties, then alphabetically by surname, then by forename, then chronologically.

A completely new Appendix 5, written by Mrs Jennifer Thorp BA, lists the Church books depositied in the Angus Library, Regent's Park College, Oxford, the principal Baptist Union archive.

I am also indebted to Mrs Faith Bowers BA MPhil, for the illustrations which enhance this new edition.

It is this author's hope that this edition may prove of even greater usefulness to researchers world-wide than its predecessors.

But theſe Lords Bs. Cannot in anie wiſe embrace one, that doth faithfully ſecke for reformation, becauſe ſuch are onely abberſaries to their kingdome. Wee ſtill pray our lord the King that wee may be free from ſuſpect, for habeing anie thoughts of provoking euill againſt them of the Romiſh religion, in regard of their profeſſion, if they be true & faithfull ſubiects to the King for wee do freely profeſſe, that our lord the King hath no more power ober their conſciences then ober ours, and that is none at all: for our lord the King is but an earthly King, and he hath no authoritie as a King but in earthly cauſes, and if the Kings people be obedient & true ſubiects, obeying all humane lawes made by the King, our lord the King can require no more: for mens religion to God, is betwixt God and themſelues; the King ſhall not anſwere for it, neither may the King be iudg betwerne God and man. Let them be hereticks, Turcks, Iewes, or whatſoeuer it apperteynes not to the earthly power to puniſh them in the leaſt meaſure. This is made euident to our lord the King by the ſcriptures. When Paul was brought before Gallio the puttie of Achaia, and accuſed of the Iewes for perſuading men to worſhip God contrary to the law, Gallio ſaid vnto the Iewes, if it were a matter of wronge or an evill deed, o ye Iewes, I would according to right mainteyne you, & he drave them from the iudgment ſeat Act. 18. 12. 17. ſhewing them that matters of wrong and euill deeds, which were betwixt man & man apperteyned onely to the iudgment ſeat, and not queſtions of religion. The like is ſhewed by the towne clarke of Epheſus in Act. 19. 38. 19. And further Paul being in like caſe accuſed of manie thinges Act. 24. in the 25. chap. he appeales to Ceſars iudgment ſeat, where he ſaith he ought to be
iij                        iudged,

# MY ANCESTORS WERE BAPTISTS

The purpose of this booklet is to enable a would-be researcher to gain biographical information concerning Baptist ancestors.

An enquiry is more likely to be successful if some preparatory work is done, and time spent in studying the contemporaneous religious and social climate can provide the background information which makes a biography so much more than an accumulation of statistics.

Before proceeding, some basic facts need to be learned. The Baptist denomination is not a 'church' in the sense that there is a Methodist Church or a Church of England. Both of these churches are centrally organised, each local church being accountable to a denominational headquarters which can provide a systemised record of their ministers and the local churches.

Each local Baptist church, by contrast, is a separate, autonomous body, self-governed by the 'church meeting', which is the decision-making body. Although there are area Associations and a Union of Baptist churches, individual churches can decide whether to join them or remain independent.

Differences in theological emphasis have also been an important factor in Baptist organisation. A brief historical outline is given in each issue of the *Baptist Union Directory* since 1973 and this currently reads:

> Organised Baptist life in England had two distinct beginnings. In 1611 Thomas Helwys led back from Amsterdam a small group who a few years earlier had sought religious freedom in Holland and who had there formed themselves into a Separatist church – under the leadership of John Smyth – practising believers' baptism. Helwys was the author of *The Mistery of Iniquity,* the first English printed book to plead for full religious freedom. The successors of Helwys and his friends became known as General Baptists. They were Arminian in theology but their church order was previously independent but modified by the appointment of intercongregational officials known as 'Messengers'.
>
> In 1633 a group connected with a Calvinistic Separatist church in London broke away on adopting believers' baptism. This was the origin of the Particular Baptists. They remained Calvinistic in theology but their church order was of the more 'independent' type. The first Baptist church in Wales was founded in 1649 at Ilston, near Swansea. Baptists had founded work in Ireland by the mid-seventeenth century and in Scotland by the

mid-eighteenth century. A 'New Connexion' of the more evangelical General Baptists was formed in 1770 under the influence of the Methodist revival by Dan Taylor; certain General Baptist churches remained aloof, however, and of these the majority became Unitarian. The late eighteenth century also witnessed a resurgence of evangelistic zeal amongst the Particular Baptists, as a result of the influence of Andrew Fuller (1754-1815) and others whose Calvinism was actively evangelical in spirit. The formation of the Baptist Missionary Society in 1792, whose first missionary William Carey went to India in 1793, was the most notable fruit of this renewal of Particular Baptist life. The influence of the BMS led in its turn to the formation in 1812-13 of the first Baptist Union amongst Particular Baptist churches. The Union had an uncertain early history, but after its re-formation in 1831-32, Particular Baptists and General Baptists of the New Connexion began to draw more closely together. This process culminated in 1891, when the General Baptists of the New Connexion, under the leadership of John Clifford (1836-1923) amalgamated with the Baptist Union.

Certain churches have remained more strictly Calvinistic, and in general have refused to receive any at the Lord's Table who have not been immersed as believers. They are known as Strict Baptists, usually, and have three regional Associations of Strict Baptist Churches. The Strict Baptist Assembly continued until 1976 when they joined the Assembly of baptised churches holding the Calvinistic doctrine of Sovereign Grace to form the Grace Baptist Assembly.

The Baptist denomination has, over the years, spread to many lands and is today one of the largest Protestant communions in the world, linked in the fellowship of the Baptist World Alliance, formed in 1905.

From this one can readily understand that there is a variety of Baptist organisation and it is necessary to discover to which emphasis the desired ancestor subscribed!

Today, many churches belong to the Baptist Union of Great Britain, but some belong to the various strands of Strict Baptist polity, more usefully classified by the name of the religious periodical whose basis of belief finds the accord of the membership, thus: *Gospel Standard* (1835 to date); *Gospel Herald* (1833-1969); *Earthen Vessel* (1845-1886); *Christian's Pathway* (1896-1969); *Grace* (1970 to date). Yet others are completely autonomous, not associated with any other church, association or grouping.

Other Baptist groupings include the Seventh-Day Baptists, whose Sabbath is observed on Saturday. Never great in numbers in this country, they are still of some importance in the United States of America.

The Scotch Baptists who began in the eighteenth century, had some influence south of the border also, and some Baptist churches in England derive from them.

_1824_

_Stroud Baptist Church_

For many years past it had been considered a desirable object to establish a Baptist Church in this town, but numerous obstacles prevented. In the year 1823 the Rev? S? Wickens having resigned his pastoral charge at Eastcombs was solicited by several Baptist friends residing in the Town to undertake this great work which invitation he kindly accepted, and a suitable piece of ground having been obtained it was, on the 25th of March 1823 conveyed to thirteen Trustees for the purpose of erecting there on a Meeting House for the use of the Baptist Denomination. On the first of July 1824 the Meeting House was opened for Divine worship when three sermons were preached. Mr Jenkin Thomas of Cheltenham Morning and Afternoon from Neh 1st Chap 39 ver and 53 Isa 10 Mr Stodhart of Pell Street London in the Even? from 2 Cor 3 Chap 9 ver, Mess?s Thomas of Wotton Sutton Baptist Missionary native of Stroud White Cirencester, Drayton Gloucester Rogers Monmouth and Richards Stonehouse / Independents / engaged

_Opening words of the Church Book, recording the foundation of_
_Stroud Baptist Church, Gloucestershire._

Of more recent origin, the Old Baptist Union which derives from the United States, began in this country in 1880 and currently numbers about thirteen churches.

The Churches of Christ, sometimes known as the Disciples of Christ, are so similar to Baptists in their belief and practice that, in the past, some of their churches have joined Baptist Associations. Nevertheless they have remained separate until quite recently when most joined the United Reformed Church.

Although the majority of Baptist churches in this country are associated with the Baptist Union, the churches retain their autonomy and may choose to send or withhold such statistical and other information which the Union seeks to enable it to compile the annual *Handbook* (now named the *Baptist Union Directory*).

The minister of each Baptist church is chosen by the members of that church, and the title 'Baptist minister' does not automatically carry with it any guarantee of theological training, doctrinal orthodoxy, ordination or accreditation. It simply denotes one who at some time is, or has been, in pastoral charge.

There are some basic introductory works of Baptist history which would well repay study before one launches upon an enquiry about a specific individual. The principal works issued during the past century are:

Whitley, W T, *A History of British Baptists,* (London 1st edn. 1923, 2nd revised edn. 1932)
Underwood, A C, *A History of the English Baptists,* (London, 1947)
McBeth, H L, *The Baptist Heritage,* (Nashville, Tennessee, U.S.A.,1987)
Payne, E A, *The Baptist Union: a Short History,* (London, 1959)
White, B R, *The English Baptists of the Seventeenth Century,* (London, 1983)
Brown, R, *The English Baptists of the Eighteenth Century,* (London, 1986)
Briggs, J H Y, *The English Baptists of the Nineteenth Century,* (London, 1994)
Bassett, T M, *The Welsh Baptists,* (Swansea, 1977)
Yuille, G, *History of the Baptists in Scotland,* (Glasgow, 1926)
Bebbington, D W, (ed.), *The Baptists in Scotland,* (Glasgow, 1988)

From previous centuries, the following two works contain a wealth of biographical information as well as individual Baptist church histories:

Crosby, T, *The History of the English Baptists* [to 1714], (4 vols., London, 1738-1740)
Ivimey, J, *A History of the English Baptists*, (4 vols., London, 1811-1830)

*The Records of a Church of Christ (1640 - 1687) were kept by Edward Terrill and cover the early years of Broadmead, Bristol. Founded in 1640 as a body of Independent Separatists, they were an open membership Baptist Church by 1653.*

From 1 July 1837 the law has required the registration of all births, marriages and deaths in England and Wales and these records are in the custody of the Registrar-General, who will issue certificates of these events. The current cost (2001) is £6.50 to callers, or £11 by post for each certificate, (only £8 if index references are quoted). The indexes alone may be searched by callers free of charge. These are records of separate events and are not linked together in families. Any correspondence about these records should be addressed to the Registrar-General, Family Records Centre, 1 Myddelton Street, London EC1R 1UW. Web site: *http://www.ons.gov.uk/*

In Scotland, civil registration began in 1855, and these records are in the custody of the Registrar-General, New Register House, Princes Street, Edinburgh EH1 3YT, who will issue certificates of these events. Whilst callers need to pay a search fee, this provides access not only to the indexes, but also to a sight of the actual entry. Postal application is also possible, but it would be wise to write initially, as the search fees are not the same as those charged in London for English and Welsh certificates. New Register House is also the repository for many older records of genealogical interest. These records may also be accessed in London from the Family Records Centre, who can give full details of the procedure.

In England and Wales before 1 July 1837, the principal means of recording births, christenings (= infant baptisms), marriages and deaths or burials were parish registers kept by clergymen of the Church of England. The best way to trace them is to contact the appropriate county archivist or the minister of the church in which the ceremony is thought to have taken place.

# BIRTHS

Births of children to Baptist parents were not automatically recorded in the parish registers. This is because Church of England parish registers relate to infant baptisms, a practice conscientiously disfavoured by Baptists. There might anyway be a considerable interval between birth and baptism. Nevertheless, an extract from such a register, termed a 'certificate of baptism' was accepted by the courts as a valid legal document, whereas Nonconformist records were usually not.

However, where the persons were of such status as to need to protect property rights, the occasional services of the Church of England were often resorted to, for security reasons, without too much hurt of conscience. One needs to remember that before the introduction of civil registration in 1837, there was an atmosphere of occasional conformity and it is difficult sometimes to divide what people were willing to do for the sake of the law from what they did out of choice.

6

Early legislation in 1695 and 1700 to combat this injustice required Dissenters' births to be reported to the incumbent either to be added to his register, or entered in a separate book. Unfortunately these laws were not universally effective, although it does explain the use of the word 'born' against some entries in baptismal registers, usually, but not exclusively, those of Nonconformists.

In other words, the parish register is the first place to look when seeking evidence of any Baptist birth which occurred before July 1837, the more especially because sometimes people changed their religious allegiance. The fact that a person was a Baptist later in life does not necessarily mean that was their confession at the time of marriage, or that they were born into a Baptist family.

Nevertheless, quite independently of parish records, Baptists quite often kept their own church's record of births, marriages and deaths. Not all churches kept records, and by no means have all survived.

Following the 1837 introduction of civil registration, the law required all these Nonconformist registers to be surrendered to the Registrar-General who was then empowered to issue from them certificates which would have the force of law. More recently these 'non-parochial registers' as they are called, passed into the custody of the Public Record Office. Today they are viewed on film at The Family Records Centre, 1 Myddelton Street, London EC1R 1UW (web site: *http://www.pro.gov.uk/*) where they are classified 'RG 4'.

Although the greatest concentration of surviving non-parochial registers is to be found at the Public Record Office, and these are all listed in a catalogue which was published by Her Majesty's Stationery Office in 1859 under the title *Lists of Non-Parochial Registers and Records in the Custody of the Registrar-General of Births, Deaths, and Marriages,* there are others which were not surrendered, partly because of the deep independence of spirit of many custodians and partly because registration was often done in Church Books which also included minutes and other records.

Indeed, these records were not always kept in the church buildings, but in the private homes of church officers. Some of these non-surrendered records have found their way to county record offices, to Baptist Church House, London (these records were removed to Regent's Park College, Oxford, in 1985), or to other repositories held by Baptist Theological Colleges or to area Associations of Baptist churches. Yet others are in the hands of the Strict Baptist Historical Society or the Gospel Standard Baptist Library, whilst some still remain in the custody of the churches to which they relate.

Since there is, as yet, no index of the whereabouts of the records of individual churches, and there is such a vast holding at the Public Record Office, search should begin there.

There is another important source of information for the period before 1837. Recognising that the Dissenters kept their own registers in a somewhat sporadic way, the Protestant Dissenting Deputies, a body that existed to protect the civil rights of the Dissenters, established a 'General Register of the Births of the Children of Protestant Dissenters of the three Denominations' (Baptist, Congregational and Presbyterian). This register of births is indexed, and commenced in 1742 (with entries for 1716 and onwards), and continued to 31 December 1837. It is now in the custody of the Public Record Office under the title of its former location, Dr Williams's Library, Red Cross Street, London [PRO reference RG 4/4666-73]. Although centralised in London, it was not limited to Londoners or to Protestant Dissenters; its tens of thousands of entries include some from outside the British Isles, and represented a considerable number of children of Baptist parents.

# MARRIAGES

The history of the marriage ceremony among Baptists, as with all Dissenters, falls into three main parts: from 1688 to 1753, from 1753 to June 1837, and since 1 July 1837. During the first period, Dissenting marriages were tolerated, though not legalised as such; in the second period they were neither tolerated nor legalised; in the third they were legalised but under conditions involving a series of stigmas and disabilities which were only removed piecemeal by steady pressure for some sixty years.

Until the passing of Lord Hardwicke's Act in 1753, marriage in Nonconformist chapels was not uncommon, for the public contract made by the parties constituted a legal marriage, though the validity of the ceremony itself was not recognised by the law. The Act, which was occasioned by the scandals of prison weddings and other irregularities was aimed not at Dissenters' marriages but at clandestine marriages. However, by making all marriages illegal in England except those regularly celebrated by the clergy of the Established Church, it removed the old common law toleration of 'irregular' marriages.

During the second period, then, Dissenters were compelled to go the Church of England (or over the border to Scotland!) if they wished to be married legally. But the clergy were not always willing to marry them, especially if they were brought up as Baptists and had not been baptised as infants.

I Thomas Bond Superintendent Registrar of the District of Stroud — in the County of Gloucester — — do hereby certify That the Building named "The Baptist Chapel" — situated at Chapel Street in the Parish of Stroud — in the County of Gloucester — having been duly certified as a place of Public Religious Worship was registered for the Solemnization of Marriage therein, on the fifteenth — day of July — in the Year of our Lord One thousand eight hundred and thirty seven—

Witness my hand this twentieth day of July — in the Year of our Lord One thousand eight hundred and thirty seven.

Thos. Bond

Superintendent Registrar

*Certificate of Place of Marriage. Superintendent Registrar's certificate that appointed the Baptist chapel in Chapel Street, Stroud, as a place for solemnization of Marriage 1837.*

In the third period, although Nonconformist ministers could conduct the ceremony, the attendance of the local civil registrar was required as the 'leading person' responsible for legal formalities and certification. It was not until 1898 that an 'authorised person' who need not be the minister, was allowed to act in the place of the Registrar.

To discover evidence of a Baptist marriage one needs to remember that there are no Nonconformist records before 1642 and few Baptist records before 1688. From 1688 to 1753, there are very few Baptist marriages recorded and from 1753 to 1837, the parish registers of the Church of England are also the most likely source.

For marriages since 1 July 1837 the information obtainable from the General Register Office can scarcely be supplemented.

# DEATHS

Parish registers of burials do not usually quote the date of death. Consequently, although the dates of death and burial are generally closer together than many dates of birth and infant baptism, the searcher needs to note that there is a time difference and accordingly a precise date of death is often not available.

Burials took place in parish churchyards except where Baptist meeting-houses had their own burial grounds. Normally, burials were recorded in parish registers when the dead were buried in the churchyard, and quite often when they were not. Anglican officials claimed that, in whatever ground the burial might be, they ought not to be defrauded of their customary fees when funerals occurred in the parish: for example, when, in 1806, the mother of a Dissenting minister at Godmanchester near Huntingdon was buried in a meeting-house ground, 'the Rev. Mr. Harris, a Dissenting minister from Cambridge, delivering an oration at the grave' a fee was demanded by the clergyman (and refused, on the advice of the Protestant Dissenting Deputies!).

In the country many Baptist churches had their own burial grounds, usually adjacent to or surrounding the church; sometimes interments occurred within the church, 'beneath the pulpit' being a not uncommon resting-place for ministers. In urban areas too, burial facilities were sometimes provided within the confines of the church building itself; such burials were termed 'intra-mural' and often the number of burials far exceeded the demands of the membership. Most chapels levied a scale of fees which were greater for non-members, and such burials provided a source of income to the church.
One infamous example was Enon Baptist Chapel, Clement's Lane, Strand, London

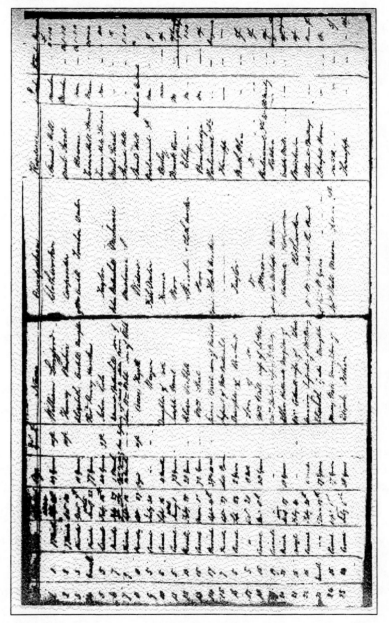

*First page of Stroud burial register.*

WC2, of which the Revd William House was minister from 1821 to 1835. This was registered for below-floor burials 1823-42, and more than 1,200 were buried there. The chapel was closed in 1842, bought by a speculator and turned into a dance hall, who issued an advertisement 'Enon Chapel – Dancing on the Dead. Admission threepence. No lady or gentleman admitted unless wearing shoes and stockings.' In 1848 the chapel became the property of a philanthropic surgeon who had all the bodies removed to Norwood Cemetery.

Apart from individual chapel burial grounds, there was a large burial ground for Nonconformists at Bunhill Fields, City Road, London EC1. The Bunhill Fields register, recording interments there from 1713 to 1854 contains over 100,000 (indexed) entries in 33 volumes, and is deposited at the Public Record Office (PRO reference to the indexes is RG 4/4652-57).

Biographical details of some hundreds of these, including many Baptists, are to be found in:

Jones, J A,        *Bunhill Memorials* (London, 1849)
Light, A W,        *Bunhill Fields* (vol. 1, 2nd edn., London, 1915, vol. 2, London, 1933)

Many Baptist chapel burial registers covering the period before 1837 are deposited in the non-parochial registers at the Public Record Office. Although records of deaths since 1 July 1837 are exhaustively covered by the Registrar-General, non-parochial registers for this period are much harder to trace. Some are still in the custody of the individual churches, some are in county record offices and some which had fallen into private hands are without trace. Fortunately, however, all these events are covered by the Registrar-General's registers of deaths.

The rapid rise of the population of England and Wales in the early nineteenth century (1801 = 9 million; 1811 = 10m; 1821 = 12m; 1831 = 13.9m; 1841 = 15.9m; 1851 = 17.9m) meant a continuing increase in the number of births, marriages and deaths, and especially in cities and large towns. One consequence of this is that the urban burial grounds of the Established Church and the Dissenters alike reached saturation point around the middle of the century, and thus urban burials from about 1850 have principally been in municipal cemeteries whose records are kept by the local authorities' registrars of cemeteries. Although these records duplicate some of the information a death certificate would give, they sometimes reveal the existence of relatives buried in the same grave, or indicate there is a memorial which may yield genealogical information.

# CENSUS RECORDS

With the exception of the year 1941 (during the Second World War), a decennial census of population has been taken continuously from 1801 to 2001. The first four censuses are only of value for general statistical purposes, but in 1841 the census included names of householders and occupants, a rough indication of age, and relationship to the head of each household of every member of the population, together with an indication of whether or not the subject was born in the county in which he/she resided at census-time. This census was completed in pencil, not always easy to decipher. From 1851 onwards, censuses were completed in ink, gave specific age and birthplace, as well as occupation, and are much more legible. No census returns within the previous hundred years are available for search at the Family Records Centre, 1 Myddelton Street, London EC1R 1UW (web site: *http://www.ons.gov.uk/*), where these records are kept, the censuses of 1841, 1851, 1861, 1871, 1881 and 1891 being currently available. A complete surname index covering all of England and Wales, for the 1881 Census, is available. The 1901 Census will also be available for search from 1 January 2002. Indexes have been compiled of the names contained in the census returns for numerous places, so a preliminary search in local libraries could well save a journey to the PRO. The very nature of the census links individuals within families and thus is of prime usefulness to genealogists and family researchers.

Uniquely, in 1851, in addition to the population census, a religious census was held, and every known church, chapel and meeting-place in England and Wales had to complete a standardised form giving church attendance on 30 March 1851, together with the date of foundation of the church and its seating capacity. The form also invited remarks, which are sometimes quite revealing. These returns were all signed by the minster or a lay leader within the church and when used in conjunction with the 1851 population census, can shed further light upon these individuals. The returns of the 1851 religious census are also held by the Public Record Office, Ruskin Avenue, Kew, Surrey TW9 4DU in class HO 159.

# BAPTIST MINISTERS

Unlike such centrally organised denominations as the Church of England, the Methodist Church, or the Salvation Army, there has never been in the Baptist denomination a single repository which even lists all past and present Baptist ministers, much less can give detailed biographical information concerning them. This is a necessary result of the autonomy of each local congregation.

There are some Baptist Ministers, and churches too, which are not allied to any association, union, or grouping with other ministers and churches, but those who are aligned in such a way may currently belong to one of these organisations:

The Baptist Union of Great Britain (formed 1812), Baptist House, P.O. Box 44, 129 Broadway, Didcot, Oxfordshire OX11 8RT. They currently publish The Baptist Union Directory, listing ministers and churches in Baptist Union membership. This has appeared annually since 1973. Its forerunners were The Baptist Handbook, 1861-1972, The Baptist Manual, 1845-59, and Account of the Proceedings of the Annual Sessions of the Baptist Union, 1832-44.

The Baptist Union of Wales (formed 1866), Ilston House, 94 Mansel Street, Swansea SA1 5TU. They publish an annual Diary and Handbook.

The Baptist Union of Scotland (formed 1869), Baptist Church House, 14 Aytoun Road, Pollokshields, Glasgow G41 5RT. They publish The Scottish Baptist Year Book.

It should be noted that Welsh and Scottish information was included in the Baptist Union publications until very recent times. Many of the churches in membership with the Baptist Unions of Wales and Scotland were also in membership with the Baptist Union of Great Britain, and their information occurred in the publications of both Unions.

The Baptist Union of Ireland, 3 FitzWilliam Street, Belfast BT9 6AW.

Grace Baptist Assembly (Secretary Mr K A Johns, 4 Beechwood Road, Caterham, Surrey CR3 6NA.) The Grace Magazine Directory of Churches is published annually and is obtainable from The Directory Secretary, 19 Croydon Road, Caterham, Surrey CR3 6PA.

Association of Grace Baptist Churches (South-East) (Secretary Mr D C Chapman, 175 Tower Bridge Road, London SE1 2AH.)

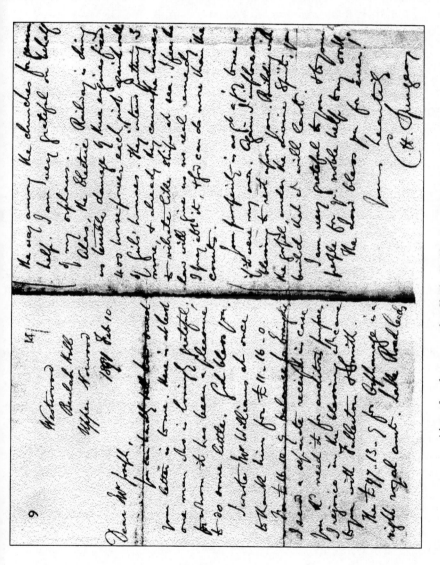

A letter from famous preacher Charles Haddon Spurgeon (1834 - 1892) held in the archives at Spurgeon's College.

Association of Grace Baptist Churches (East Midlands) (Secretary Mr A B Keen, 1 Cemetery Road, Whittlesey, Cambs. PE7 1SF.)

Association of Grace Baptist Churches (East Anglia) (Administrator Mr D J Piper, Dunoon, Top Road, Rattlesden, Bury St Edmunds, Suffolk IP30 OSJ.)

The Gospel Standard (Strict Baptist, formed 1835) 'List of Chapels and Ministers' Engagements' is published monthly in the *Gospel Standard*. The current producer of this list is Mr J L Rosier, 1 Wheatsheaf Close, Loose Road, Maidstone, Kent, ME15 9QA.

The Old Baptist Union (formed 1880) (Secretary, Reverend C N Whiteley, 64 Kennedy Avenue, Macclesfield, Cheshire SK10 3DE). Current membership about thirteen churches and one in the Netherlands. Most of these churches joined the Baptist Union of Great Britain in November 1993, and are now formed as an Association within it.

General Baptist Assembly [Inc] (Secretary Mr L J Maguire, 2 The Twitten, Ditchling, Hassocks, East Sussex BN6 8UJ).

Some Baptist ministers and churches are in membership of the Fellowship of Independent Evangelical Churches, 3 Church Road, Croydon, Surrey CR0 1SG.

This list does not claim to be complete, but it does give some idea of the diversity of attachment and association of the various churches and ministers, all calling themselves 'Baptist'.

It will be noted that most of the organisations mentioned date from the nineteenth century. The sources of information concerning Baptist ministers and churches of the seventeenth and eighteenth centuries are diverse and include 'Church Books' as the minute books of the churches were generally called, the non-parochial registers, many of which are in the Public Record Office, to which reference has already been made, and the church histories, memorials and monumental inscriptions on gravestones, where these are still extant. Here the county record offices can often help with local background information which adds much interest to the research.

There have been several attempts to list Baptist ministers:

In 1715, Dr John Evans, a Presbyterian, compiled lists of Dissenting congregations in England and Wales, by counties, with names of ministers and some additional information. These lists, with corrections and additions down to 1729, are held by Dr Williams's Library, 14 Gordon Square, London WC1H 0AG, under library reference MS.35.4.

In 1753, the Revd John Collett Ryland wrote an account of the Baptist churches in London, etc. This is to be found in the Warwick Baptist Church minute book, written by Ryland himself when he was minister there. This contains biographical information of 146 Particular Baptist ministers, and a transcript appears in *Transactions of the Baptist Historical Society,* vol. 6 (1919) pp. 138-57. This is the first part of an article entitled 'Baptist Ministers in England about 1750 A.D'; the second part (on pages 157-62) gives a list of General Baptist ministers.

In 1763, the Particular Baptist Fund in London printed a list of Baptist churches and minsters in England, arranged by counties. Based upon Ryland's list of 1753, it included information from other sources. A transcript of this list appears in Ivimey, J, *A History of the English Baptists*, vol. 4 (1830) pp. 13-21.

In 1773, the Revd Josiah Thompson, a Baptist, produced lists (similar to Dr John Evans' of 1715) by counties, for the years 1715 and 1773. These are available in Dr Williams's Library, reference MS.35.5.

From 1790 to 1802, Dr John Rippon produced one of the earliest Baptist periodicals, entitled *The Baptist Annual Register*, which ran to four volumes. During this period, he produced three lists, by counties, of the Particular Baptist churches in England and Wales, with their ministers. The 1790 list appears in vol. 1 on pages 3-16. the 1794 list is in vol. 2, pp. 1-24, and that for 1798 in vol. 3, pp. 1-43. There is a wealth of biographical information in the footnotes to these lists, as well as biographical studies and obituaries elsewhere in this work.

Walter Wilson (1781-1847) produced in four volumes published between 1808 and 1814 *The History and Antiquities of Dissenting Churches and Meeting Houses in London, Westminster and Southwark, Including the Lives of their Ministers,* which, although geographically restricted contains valuable biographies of many Baptist ministers.

*The Baptist Magazine*, which began in 1809, continued from time to time, listings in the same form as Rippon. These are:

1811, pp. 458-63 (England); pp. 496-97 (Wales)
1823, pp. 23-29, 159-62, 331-32, 432-34 (England only)
1827, pp. 32-35, 80-83, 135-39 (England only)
1831, pp. 160-64, 203-07, (England); pp. 499-503 (Wales); pp. 503-04 (Scotland); pp. 590-97 an alphabetical list of Particular Baptist ministers in England; p. 598 General Baptist ministers in England; p. 599 list of Baptist missionaries.
1835, pp. 549-66 Evangelical Baptist churches in England (includes both Particular and General).

*The New Baptist Miscellany* contains on pages 23-32 of the 1831 volume, a 'List of Baptist Churches [at the end of 1830] with the date of their commencement, the names of their ministers, and the year of their settlement'.

It will be noticed that there is a list of General Baptist ministers (of the New Connexion) in the 1831 *Baptist Magazine.* The General Baptists had two able historians who produced works which list all the General Baptist churches of the New Connexion and their ministers, and contain a wealth of biographical material. These are:

Taylor, Adam, *The History of the English General Baptists* (2 vols., London, 1818) Wood, J H, *A Condensed History of the General Baptists of the New Connexion* (London, 1847)

The New Connexion of General Baptists published Minutes of their Annual Associations from 1770 to 1869. This title was then changed to *The General Baptist Year Book,* which appeared annually from 1870 to 1891. All of these contain valuable listings of ministers and churches.

The Minutes of the General Baptists who did not join the New Connexion contain much useful information about churches, as well as their ministers and lay delegates, in Whitley, W T, *Minutes of the General Assembly of the General Baptist Churches in England,* 1654-1728 and 1731-1811 (2 vols., London, 1909-10).

Although during the period 1832-44, an *Account of the Proceedings of the Annual Sessions of the Baptist Union* was published each year, lists of churches and ministers appeared only in those for the years 1836, 1838, 1840, 1843 and 1844. This publication changed its title to *A Manual of the Baptist Denomination*, and lists of churches and ministers appeared annually from 1845 to 1859.

No annual alphabetical list of ministers appeared during the twenty years following that in the *Baptist Magazine* for 1831. However, production of this list was resumed in the December Supplement to the *Baptist Magazine* for 1851 and this practice continued annually until 1860.

The *Baptist Handbook* which began in 1861 appeared annually until 1972 after which it changed its name to the *Baptist Union Directory*, and is still published. This contains a list of churches, by counties (latterly Baptist Association Areas) and also ministers, alphabetically.

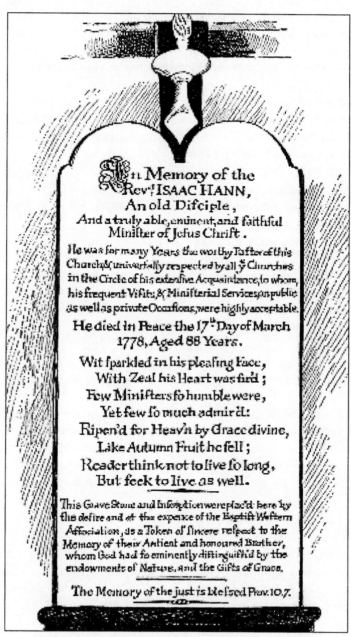

In Memory of the
Rev.ᵈ ISAAC HANN,
An old Difciple,
And a truly able, eminent, and faithful
Minifter of Jefus Chrift.

He was for many Years the worthy Paftor of this
Church,&(univerfally refpected by all y Churches
in the Circle of his extenfive Acquaintance, to whom,
his frequent Vifits, & Minifterial Services on public
as well as private Occafions, were highly acceptable.

He died in Peace the 17ᵗʰ Day of March
1778, Aged 88 Years.

Wit fparkled in his pleafing Face,
With Zeal his Heart was fir'd;
Few Minifters fo humble were,
Yet few fo much admir'd:
Ripen'd for Heav'n by Grace divine,
Like Autumn Fruit he fell;
Reader think not to live fo long,
But feek to live as well.

This Grave Stone and Infcription were plac'd here by
the defire and at the expence of the Baptift Weftern
Affociation, as a Token of fincere refpect to the
Memory of their Antient and honoured Brother,
whom God had fo eminently diftinguifh'd by the
endowments of Nature, and the Gifts of Grace.

The Memory of the just is bleffed Prov. 10. 7.

*Memorial stone for the Revd. Isaac Hann (1747 - 1778), the most
celebrated pastor of the Church. This is a rare example of an interment
inside a non-conformist chapel.*

The Baptist Historical Society maintains a consolidated list of all the obituaries which have appeared in the *Baptist Union Directory,* the *Baptist Handbook,* the *Manual of the Baptist Denomination,* the *Account of the Proceedings* and <u>some</u> of those which have appeared in the *Baptist Magazine.* Application should be made to the Secretary.

There are other listings of ministers to which reference may usefully be made; the Baptist Theological Colleges have all, at some time, published lists of former students, and these usually state the student's home church, his date of joining or leaving college and his location when the list was published.

Although earlier listings did not include this information, one may find what college, if any, a minister attended, from any *Baptist Handbook* issued in 1869 or subsequently.

Many of the listings already mentioned include the name of the county or area Association to which a church belongs. Each of these Associations publishes an annual *Yearbook* or *Handbook* which contains statistical information concerning churches and ministers. Although much of this is duplicated in the national listings, they sometimes provide additional facts.

The Baptist Missionary Society was formed in 1792, and a list of missionaries from the formation of the Society was issued as an appendix to the Centenary volume of the Baptist Missionary Society, published in 1892. This list is on pages 313-29.

Quite a number of ministers also wrote books and some of them, hymns. There are standard dictionaries of hymnology, of which that by J Julian is best known, and many hymnbooks have a companion volume which gives biographies of the writers.

Amongst the works of Baptist bibliography, two stand pre-eminent:

> Whitley, W T, *A Baptist Bibliography:* vol. 1 1526-1776 (London, 1916), and vol. 2 1777-1837, with addenda from 1613 (London, 1922). These books have been out of print for many years but were re-published in one volume in 1985. A third volume was projected, but never published.
> Starr, E C, *A Baptist Bibliography,* 25 vols. (American Baptist Historical Society, Rochester, New York, U.S.A., 1947-76).

( 74 )

fmall a number would, upon receiving the firft crop, maintain themfelves. They would have the advantage of choofing their fituation, their wants would be few; the women, and even the children, would be neceffary for domeftic purpofes; and a few articles of flock, as a cow or two, and a bull, and a few other cattle of both fexes, a very few utenfils of hufbandry, and fome corn to fow their land, would be fufficient. Thofe who attend the miffionaries fhould underftand hufbandry, fifhing, fowling, &c. and be provided with the neceffary implements for thefe purpofes. Indeed a variety of methods may be thought of, and when once the work is undertaken, many things will fuggeft themfelves to us, of which we at prefent can form no idea.

FIRSTLY, As to *learning their language*, the fame means would be found neceffary here as in trade between different nations. In fome cafes interpreters might be obtained, who might be employed for a time; and where thefe were not to be found, the miffionaries muft have patience, and mingle with the people, till they have learned fo much of their language as to be able to communicate their ideas to them in it It is well known to require no very extraordinary talents to learn, in the fpace of a year, or two at moft, the language of any people upon earth, fo much

of

( 75 )

of it at leaft, as to be able to convey any fentiments we wifh to their underftandings.

The Miffionaries muft be men of great piety, prudence, courage, and forbearance; of undoubted orthodoxy in their fentiments, and muft enter with all their hearts into the fpirit of their miffion; they muft be willing to leave all the comforts of life behind them, and to encounter all the hardfhips of a torrid, or a frigid climate, an uncomfortable manner of living, and every other inconvenience that can attend this undertaking. Clothing, a few knives, powder and fhot, fifhing-tackle, and the articles of hufbandry above-mentioned, muft be provided for them; and when arrived at the place of their deftination, their firft bufinefs muft be to gain fome acquaintance with the language of the natives, (for which purpofe two would be better than one,) and by all lawful means to endeavour to cultivate a friendfhip with them, and as foon as poffible let them know the errand for which they were fent. They muft endeavour to convince them that it was their good alone, which induced them to forfake their friends, and all the comforts of their native country. They muft be very careful not to refent injuries which may be offered to them, nor to think highly of themfelves, fo as to defpife the poor heathens, and by thofe means lay a foundation

L

for

*Pages from William Carey's An Enquiry into the Obligations of Christians to use Means for the Conversion of the Heathen (1792), a blueprint for the first Missionary Society.*

# CHURCH MEMBERS

Apart from the information in the non-parochial registers, in the Public Record Office, of which a complete list of the Baptist ones is given in Appendix 1, the *Church Minute Books* of each church, if available, are an important source of information. Nevertheless, in these, Christian names are usually given as initials or omitted altogether, and are only included with reference to some specific action performed by, or required of, the individual concerned. This generally means that only a small minority (often the most vocal!) have their names recorded in the minutes.

Church Books, however often contain a membership list, which can be most useful, as there is sometimes an address or an indication of married surnames of ladies whose membership started when they were single.

The first place to seek a Church Book is in the church itself, failing which the local reference library or county record office. Some records have been deposited with area Associations, and many are in Baptist Theological College libraries and the libraries of the Strict Baptist Historical Society and that of the Gospel Standard Baptists. All those formerly with the Baptist Union are now at Regent's Park College, Pusey Street, Oxford OX1 2LB. These are listed in Appendix 5.

A word of caution is necessary here; where church records are deposited with college libraries, staffing levels do not usually permit their availability for genealogical research. Regrettably, many Church Books have, over the centuries, fallen into private hands and some have been lost.

Individual church members do, however, find mention in many of the Baptist periodicals of which a significant number is detailed in Taylor, R, *English Baptist Periodicals,* 1790-1865, originally published in the *Baptist Quarterly,* vol. 27 (April 1977), pp. 49-82. A further reprint of this article may be available from the Treasurer of the Baptist Historical Society at £1 plus postage (The Revd T S H Elwyn M.A., B.Sc, B.D., 28 Dowthorpe Hill, Earls Barton, Northampton, NN6 0PB). In addition to periodicals mentioned earlier in this booklet, the *Baptist Times,* published weekly, contains many details of church members.

A most valuable compendium is the *National Index of Parish Registers,* under various general editors, and published in several volumes by the Society of Genealogists. Not all the volumes have been published, but those so far issued are:

| vol. | 1 | General Sources before 1837 [2002] |
|---|---|---|
| vol. | 2 | Nonconformist Sources [2002] |
| vol. | 3 | Roman Catholic and Jewish Genealogy [2002] |
| vol. | 4 | Part 1 Surrey [parts relating to Kent and Sussex are out of print] |
| vol. | 5 | Gloucestershire, Herefordshire, Oxfordshire, Shropshire, Warwickshire and Worcestershire [out of print] |
| vol. | 6 | part 1 Staffordshire |
| vol. | 6 | part 2 Nottinghamshire |
| vol. | 7 | Cambridgeshire, Norfolk, Suffolk |
| vol. | 8 | part 1 Berkshire |
| vol. | 8 | part 2 Wiltshire |
| vol. | 9 | part 1 Bedfordshire, Huntingdonshire |
| vol. | 9 | part 2 Northamptonshire |
| vol. | 9 | part 3 Buckinghamshire |
| vol. | 9 | part 4 Essex |
| vol. | 11 | part 1 Northumberland and Durham [out of print] |
| vol. | 12 | Scottish Genealogy and Family History [out of print] |
| vol. | 13 | Parish Registers of Wales (does not include nonconformist material) |

The second volume, *Sources for Nonconformist Genealogy and Family History,* is especially useful in suggesting lines of approach.

There are now many local and regional family history societies producing literature and offering guidance to the amateur. The Society of Genealogists could direct you to the most appropriate local family history society.

Often, the published histories of individual churches give useful information about ministers and members. The most accessible collection of these histories is to be found at Dr Williams's Library, London, which, in 1973, published a list of them in *Nonconformist Congregations in Great Britain.*

Not all Baptists stayed within the shores of the United Kingdom, and many ministers and members emigrated. The *Baptist Handbook* during the period 1879-1916 contained lists of overseas churches and ministers. The tracing of Baptists who emigrated to the

# ADDITIONS TO THE CHURCH.

| No. | NAME. | CIRCUMSTANCES OF ADMISSION. | DATE |
|---|---|---|---|
| 73 | Alfred Bird | By Letter from Hammersmith | Nov. 1849 |
| 74 | Emily Bird | By Letter from Hammersmith | Nov. 1849 |
| 75 | Elizabeth Phillips | By profession on conversion | Nov. 1849 |
| 76 | John W Edwards | By profession on conversion | Nov. 1849 |
| 77 | Edmund Padden | By profession on conversion | Nov. 1849 |
| 78 | Charles Braden | By profession on conversion | Nov. 1849 |
| 79 | William Wells | By profession on conversion | Nov. 1849 |
| 80 | Margaret Smith | By letter from Tottenham Court | Nov. 1849 |
| 81 | Mary Wright | By recommendation of deputation | Nov. 1849 |
| 82 | Hannah Wood | By Letter from Camden Town | Nov. 1849 |
| 83 | Elizabeth Morgan | By Letter from Devonshire Square | Dec. 1849 |
| 84 | Richard Gainham | By Letter from Carlisle | Dec. 1849 |

*These entries in the Register for Bloomsbury Chapel show people who joined the church and which church they transferred from. 'By profession on conversion' implies believer's baptism.*

# REMOVALS FROM THE CHURCH.

| MODE OF REMOVAL. | DATE. | GENERAL OBSERVATIONS. |
| By dismission | Septr. 1854 | He removed to Camberwell. |
| By dismission | Septr. 1854 | She removed to Camberwell. |
| By resignation | October 1853 | |
| By dismission | July. 1850. | He removed to Islington Green. |
| By long absence | Feby. 1857 | |
| By general dismissl. | March 1859 | Long absence. |
| By death | April. 1854 | |
| By general dismission | June 1855 | |
| By death. | August. 1850 | Her end was peace. |
| By dismission | June 1860 | She removed, as Mrs. Jones, to Woolwich. |
| By death | Jany. 1873 | |
| By dismission. | July. 1859 | He removed to Camden Road. |

*Removals are explained by death, resignation, transfer to another church,

Americas or Australasia is possible through the emigration lists published. Various lists of passengers who settled in the English colonies in America have been published.

There was a considerable Welsh emigration in the early and late eighteenth century, which has been carefully studied, and again lists are available. As they hold a large number of published emigration lists, any enquiry concerning emigrants should first be directed to the Society of Genealogists, 14 Charterhouse Buildings, Goswell Road, London EC1M 7BA.

Finally, careful reading of Amanda Bevan, *Tracing Your Ancestors in the Public Record Office* (6th edition, 2002), will save much time and wasted effort and possibly suggest further avenues of enquiry.

Those whose interest in Baptist history has been awakened may wish to extend their knowledge by joining one or both of the historical societies:
>   The Baptist Historical Society (formed 1908): Secretary, Revd S L Copson, B.A., M Litt.,60 Strathmore Avenue, Hitchin, Hertfordshire SG5 1ST.
>   The Strict Baptist Historical Society (formed 1961): Secretary, Revd Dr. K Dix, 38 Frenchs Avenue, Dunstable, Beds. LU6 1BH.

*The founding Resolution of Bloomsbury Baptist Church (1849) was signed by all 62 who were present.*

# APPENDIX 1

## A COMPLETE LIST OF THE BAPTIST REGISTERS AND RECORDS IN THE CUSTODY OF THE PUBLIC RECORD OFFICE, MADE AVAILABLE AT THE FAMILY RECORDS CENTRE, 1 MYDDELTON STREET, LONDON ECIR IUW

The numbers in the first column are the former given numbers of each register.

The W numbers in square brackets in the third column relate to the number allocated to the chapel in Whitley, W T, *The Baptists of London* (London 1928).

\* The foundation dates are as stated in the Certificate to the Commissioners when the registers were originally surrendered.

|  | **BEDFORDSHIRE** | **Founded\*** |  |  | **RG 4/** |
|---|---|---|---|---|---|
| 4 | BEDFORD<br>Mill Street | 1796 | Births | 1792-1837 | 273 |
| 7 | BIGGLESWADE | 1771 | Births<br>Burials | 1762-1837 }<br>1786-1829 } | 309 |
| 9 | BLUNHAM | 1724 | Births<br>Burials | 1709-1837 }<br>1793-1828 } | 311 |
| 10 | CARDINGTON<br>Cotton End Chapel<br>Independent & Baptist | 1777 | Births &<br>Baptisms } | 1784-1837 | 274 |
| 11 | CRANFIELD<br>Dissolved, and<br>reformed 1776 | 1662 | Births<br>Burials | 1799-1837<br>1794-1837 | 220 |
| 12 | DUNSTABLE<br>and HOUGHTON<br>REGIS<br>formerly THORN | 1801 }<br>1804 }<br>1751 | Births &<br>Burials } | 1769-1836 | 221 |
| 16 | LUTON | 1670 | Births<br>Burials<br>Burials | 1772-1837 }<br>1785-1837 }<br>1837-54 | 276<br>90 |

| | | Founded* | | | RG 4/ |
|---|---|---|---|---|---|
| 18 | MAULDEN<br>Independent<br>and Baptist | 1700 | Births<br>Burials | 1730-1837 }<br>1785-97 } | 227 |
| 20 | RIDGMONT | 1811 | Births<br>Burials | 1761-1837 }<br>1828 } | 228 |
| 22 | SHEFFORD<br>HARDWICK | 1825 | Birth | 1828-36 | 229 |
| 24 | SOUTHILL | 1693 | Births<br>Burials | 1783-1837 }<br>1802-20 } | 279 |
| 26 | WESTONING | 1816 | Births | 1798-1837 | 91 |
| 28 | WOOTTON | 1828 | Births | 1823-36 | 2392 |

**BERKSHIRE**

| | | Founded* | | | RG 4/ |
|---|---|---|---|---|---|
| 1 | ABINGDON<br>Lower Meeting House,<br>Ock Street | 1640 | Births<br>Burials<br>Births<br>Burials<br>Births<br>Burials | 1764-67 }<br>1764-89 }<br>1786-1824 }<br>1785-1828 }<br>1797-1837 }<br>1828-37 } | 231<br><br>280<br><br>312 |
| 14 | NEWBURY<br>Northcroft Lane<br>Meeting House | 1700 | Births &<br>Baptisms }<br>Births &<br>Burials<br>Baptisms | 1712-1824<br><br>1824-37<br>1835 | 87<br><br>286<br>86 |
| 18 | READING<br>King's Road<br>Meeting House,<br>formerly<br>Hosier's Lane | Reign of<br>Henry VIII | Births<br>Burials | 1819-37<br>1785-1835 | 287<br>1761 |

| | | Founded* | | | RG 4/ |
|---|---|---|---|---|---|
| 26 | WALLINGFORD | | | | |
| | Thames Street | 1794 | Births & Baptisms } | 1794-1816 | 237 |
| | | | Baptisms & Burials } | 1814-37 | 288 |

### BUCKINGHAMSHIRE

| | | Founded* | | | RG 4/ |
|---|---|---|---|---|---|
| 1 | AMERSHAM | | | | |
| | Lower Meeting House | 1783 | Births | 1773-1837 } | 239 |
| | | | Burials | 1784-1837 } | |
| 9 | CHALFONT ST PETER | | | | |
| | Gold Hill Chapel | 1780 | Baptisms | 1782-1802 } | 243 |
| | | | Burials | 1782-89 } | |
| | | | Births | 1779-1836 | 412 |
| | | | Burials | 1821-36 | 413 |
| 11 | CHENIES | 1760 | Births | 1783-1812 } | 244 |
| | | | Burials | 1787-1812 } | |
| 13 | CHESHAM | | | | |
| | Old Meeting House | 1719 | Births & Baptisms } | 1783-1823 | 249 |
| | | | Births | 1823-36 | 2662 |
| | | | Burials | 1810-27 | 2093 |
| | | | Burials | 1828-37 | 252 |
| | | | Burials | 1837 | 251 |
| 14 | CHESHAM | | | | |
| | Blucher Street | 1710 | Births & Baptisms } | 1786-1802 | 2399 |
| 19 | HADDENHAM | 1810 | Burials | 1823-37 | 2088 |

| | | Founded* | | | RG 4/ |
|---|---|---|---|---|---|
| 24 | NEWPORT PAGNELL<br>Lower Meeting | Reign of<br>Charles II | Births | 1810-37 | 147 |
| 25 | OLNEY | 1694 | Births | 1789-1837 | 257 |
| 26 | PRINCES RISBOROUGH<br>Upper Chapel | 1707 | Births | 1804-37 | 148 |
| 29 | WESTCOTT<br>parish of Waddesdon | 1833 | Births | 1834-37 | 259 |
| 30 | WINGRAVE<br>Independent<br>and Baptist | | Births &<br>Baptisms } | 1817-37 | 260 |

**CAMBRIDGESHIRE**

| | | | | | |
|---|---|---|---|---|---|
| 9 | CHATTERIS<br>Mill End | 1778 | Births &<br>Baptisms } | 1778-1821 | 2252 |
| 17 | GAMLINGAY | 1710 | Births | 1815-36 | 151 |
| 19 | ISLEHAM | 1812 | Births | 1789-1837 | 152 |
| 23 | MARCH, ISLE OF ELY<br>Bevill's Chapel<br>Calvinistic Baptist | 1807 | Births | 1805-37 | 153 |
| 24 | MARCH | 1700 | Births | 1798-1837 | 154 |

[also 32 separate Certificates, signed by witnesses, relating to 32 of the above entries]

| | | Founded* | | | RG 4/ |
|---|---|---|---|---|---|
| 30 | WHITTLESEY, ISLE OF ELY | | | | |
| | | 1821 | Births | 1810-37 | 3541 |
| 31 | WISBECH | | | | |
| | Ely Place | about time of Protectorate | Deaths & Burials } | 1818-37 | 2253 |
| 32 | WISBECH | | | | |
| | St Peter's Upper Hill Street, late Ship Lane | 1794 | Births Deaths & Burials } | 1790-1836 | 1880 |
| 34 | WISBECH | | | | |
| | Unitarian Baptist St Peter's, Church Lane, formerly Dead Man's Lane | | Births Burial } | 1783-1837 1831 | 3362 |

**CHESHIRE**

| | | | | | |
|---|---|---|---|---|---|
| 52 | NANTWICH | | | | |
| | Barker Street | 1700 | Births | 1781-1835 | 189 |
| 57a | STALEY BRIDGE: see **LANCASHIRE** RG 4/1164, 2439 | | | | |
| 76 | TARPORLEY | 1817 | Births | 1801-36 | 424 |

**CORNWALL**

| | | | | | |
|---|---|---|---|---|---|
| 17 | HELSTON | | | | |
| | Coinage Hall Street | 1805 | Births | 1814-37 | 427 |
| 30 | PADSTOW | 1834 | Births | 1836 | 106 |
| 55 | SCILLY ISLES | | | | |
| | St Mary's | 1818 | Births | 1819-37 | 204 |

|  |  | **Founded*** |  |  | **RG 4/** |
|---|---|---|---|---|---|
| 63 | TRURO | | | | |
|  | Kenwyn Street | 1789 | Births | 1760-1837 | 682 |
|  | **CUMBERLAND** | | | | |
| 11 | MARYPORT | | | | |
|  | High Street | 1808 | Births | 1797-1836 | 836 |
|  | **DERBYSHIRE** | | | | |
| 19 | DERBY | | | | |
|  | Brook Street Chapel | 1791 | Births | 1789-1808 | 694A |
|  |  |  | Births | 1809-37 | 695 |
| 38 | ILKESTON | 1785 | Births | 1773-1808 | |
|  |  |  | Baptisms | | 2156 |
|  |  |  | & Burials | 1792 | |
|  |  |  | Births | 1807-35 | 708 |
| 47 | MELBOURNE | 1750 | Births | 1753-1806 | 507 |
|  |  |  | Births | 1786-1837 | 945 |
|  |  |  | Births | 1809-37 | 946 |
|  |  |  | Burials | 1792-1837 | 118 |
| 61 | WIRKSWORTH | 1816 | Births | 1802-37 | 3519 |
|  | **DEVONSHIRE** | | | | |
| 1 | APPLEDORE | | | | |
|  | Ebenezer Chapel | 1835 | Births | 1831-37 | 950 |
| - | ASHWATER | | Births | 1828-37 | |
|  |  |  | [Unauthenticated Register RG 8/5] | | |

|     |                      | **Founded\*** |                              |           | **RG 4/** |
|-----|----------------------|---------------|------------------------------|-----------|-----------|
| 15  | BAMPTON<br>High Street | 1690 | Births<br>Baptisms<br>& Burials } | 1807-36 | 957 |
| 7   | BARNSTAPLE<br>Ebenezer Chapel | 1817 | Births | 1821-37 | 953 |
| 13  | BOVEY TRACEY<br>Hen Street Chapel | 1773 | Births &<br>Burials } | 1778-1833 | 956 |
| 17  | BRAYFORD | 1820 | Births | 1831-37 | 607 |
| 33  | CROYDE | 1824 | Births | 1821-35 | 944 |
| 34  | CULMSTOCK<br>Prescott Meeting | 1718 | Births &<br>Baptisms } | 1787-1836 | 523 |
| 38  | DEVONPORT<br>Morice Square Chapel | 1784 | Births &<br>Baptisms } | 1770-1837 | 960 |
| -   | DEVONPORT<br>Morice Square | | Baptisms 1785-94 }<br>Burials 1781-1806 }<br>[Unauthenticated Register RG 8/10] | | |
| 43  | DEVONPORT<br>Liberty Street and<br>Pembroke Street | | Births | 1779-1821 | 963 |
| 46  | DODBROOK<br>the Refuge Chapel | 1819 | Births | 1824-36 | 2533 |

| | | Founded* | | | | RG 4/ |
|---|---|---|---|---|---|---|
| 47 | EXETER South Street | 1600 | Births Baptisms & Burials | } | 1785-1837 | 964 |
| 48 | EXETER Bartholomew Street | 1817 | Births | | 1817-37 | 335 |
| 56 | HONITON | 1812 | Births | | 1829-37 | 2027 |
| 61 | KENTISBEARE Saints Hill Meeting | 1814 | Births | | 1806-36 | 337 |
| 62 | KINGSBRIDGE | 1650 | Births & Burials Burials | } | 1785-1831 1835-57 | 2099 442 |
| 73 | PLYMOUTH How Street Chapel | 1637 | Births Burials | | 1786-1837 1787-1837 | 1215 1216 |
| 92 | STONEHOUSE Ebenezer Chapel, Union Street | 1815 | Births | | 1817-37 | 2854 |
| 101 | TIVERTON Newport Street | 1687 | Births Burials | | 1767-1837 1816-37 } | 1221 |

**DORSETSHIRE**

| | | | | | |
|---|---|---|---|---|---|
| 15 | LANGTON | 1832 | Births | 1833-37 | 461 |
| 17A | LYME REGIS | 1823 | Burials | 1823-57 | 463 |
| 22 | POOLE Hill Street | 1815 | Births | 1797-1837 | 2411 |

| 35 | WEYMOUTH, MELCOMBE REGIS | | | | |
| | Bank Buildings | 1813 | Births | 1810-37 | 350 |

| 38 | WIMBORNE MINSTER | 1787 | Births | 1778-1834 | 470 |

**DURHAM**

| 24 | HAMSTERLEY | 1665 | Births & Baptisms | 1750-1837 | |
| | | | Burials | 1785-1837 | 1236 |

| 29 | MIDDLETON-IN-TEESDALE | | | | |
| | Hude Street Chapel | 1828 | Births | 1824-36 | 351 |

| 34 | ROWLEY | | | | |
| | Parish of Muggleswick | 1700 | Births | 1778-1836 | 3557 |

(Also contains entries for two chapels in **NORTHUMBERLAND**)

| 39 | SOUTH SHIELDS | | | | |
| | Barrington Street | 1818 | Births | 1809-36 | 1096 |

| 50 | SUNDERLAND | 1797 | Births | 1797-1837 | 3556 |

**ESSEX**

| 11 | CHELMSFORD | | | | |
| | Duke Street | 1802 | Births & Namings | 1793-1837 | 2161 |

| 17 | COLCHESTER | | | | |
| | New Meeting, | 1814 | Births | 1798-1837 | 1507 |
| | Stanwell Street, | dissolved | Burials | 1814-37 | 356 |
| | formerly Baptist | about 1825 | | | |
| | and Independent | | | | |

| 20 | COLCHESTER<br>Eld Lane | 1720 | Births<br>Burials<br>Burials | 1767-1837 }<br>1788-1807 }<br>1816-37 | 1510<br>801 |
|----|----|----|----|----|----|
| 31 | HARLOW | 1668 | Births<br>Burials | 1778-1839 }<br>1819-37 } | 1514 |
| 37 | LANGHAM | 1755 | Burials | 1782-1826 | 359 |
| 40 | LOUGHTON | 1817 | Births<br>Burials | 1820-37<br>1817-37 | 1517<br>1518 |
| 53 | SAFFRON WALDEN<br>Little Meeting House | 1819 | Births<br>Burials | 1802-36 }<br>1822-36 } | 786 |
| 55 | SAFFRON WALDEN<br>Upper Meeting,<br>Bailey's Lane | 1774 | Births &<br>Namings }<br>Burials | 1776-1837<br>1821-37 | 1381<br>1521 |
| 56 | SAFFRON WALDEN<br>Little Meeting | 1726 | Births<br>Burials<br>Births<br>Burials | 1790-1824 }<br>1791-1822 }<br>1826-37<br>1827-37 | 785<br>784<br>783 |
| 67 | THORPE-LE-SOKEN | 1802 | Births | 1798-1837 | 2420 |
| 72 | WALTHAM ABBEY<br>Paradise Row | 1729 | Births<br>Burials<br>Deaths<br>Burials<br>Burials | 1799-1818 }<br>1825-37 }<br>1770-1831<br>1836-37<br>1845-57 | 2291<br>778<br>2292<br>1383 |

**GLOUCESTERSHIRE**

| 6 | BLAKENEY | 1833 | Burials | 1834-37 | 3568 |
|----|----|----|----|----|----|

The births have been registered at Dr Williams's Library

| | | Founded* | | | RG 4/ |
|---|---|---|---|---|---|
| 7 | BOURTON-ON-THE WATER | 1650 | Births | 1726-1836 | |
| | | | Burials | 1801-36 } | 384 |
| 14 | CHIPPING CAMDEN | | Births | 1785-1837 | |
| | | | Baptisms | 1729-66 } | 773 |
| 16 | CIRENCESTER Coxwell Street | 1651 | Births & Baptisms } Burials | 1651-1837 1736-1839 } | 3756 |
| 22 | EASTCOMBE Stroudwater | 1800 | Births | 1797-1824 | 2296 |
| 30 | HAWKESBURY Hillsley Street | 1730 | Births Burials | 1785-1837 1767-1837 } | 2104 |
| 31 | HORSLEY Shortwood Meeting House | 1715 | Births Births | 1749-87 1787-1806 | 2297 767 |
| 49 | STOW-ON-THE-WOLD | 1716 | Births | 1821-37 | 759 |
| 50 | STROUD | 1824 | Births | 1805-37 | 621 |
| 61 | WOOTTON-UNDER-EDGE | 1717 | Births | 1784-1813 | 3564 |

**HAMPSHIRE**

| | | Founded* | | | RG 4/ |
|---|---|---|---|---|---|
| 9A | CARISBROOKE, ISLE OF WIGHT | 1809 | Burials | 1853-58 | 2107 |
| 19 | FORTON near Gosport | 1811 | Births | 1799-1836 | 400 |
| 23 | HAMBLEDON Anmore Chapel | 1827 | Births | 1820-37 | 2109 |

| | | **Founded\*** | | | **RG 4/** |
|---|---|---|---|---|---|
| 28 | LYNDHURST | | Births | 1783-1810 | } 2302 |
| | | | Burials | 1794-1835 | |
| | | | | | |
| 32 | NEWPORT, ISLE OF WIGHT | | | | |
| | Castle Hold | 1812 | Births | 1807-37 | 402 |
| | | | | | |
| 30 | NEWPORT, ISLE OF WIGHT | | | | |
| | 30 High Street, | 1739 | Baptisms | 1739-1828 | 36 |
| | Presbyterian | | Births and | 1828-1837 | 42 |
| | Formerly General Baptist | | Baptisms | | |
| | | | | | |
| 37 | PORTSEA | | | | |
| | White's Row | 1782 | Births | 1817-37 | 562 |
| | | | | | |
| 39 | PORTSEA | 1704 | Births | 1730-1803 | 1806 |
| | Meeting House Alley | | Births | 1775-1837 | 403 |
| | | | | | |
| 44 | PORTSMOUTH | 1714 | Births & | 1785-1837 | |
| | St Thomas | | Burials | 1785-1837 | 2304 |
| | | | | | |
| 51 | ROMSEY | | Births | 1808-37 | } 609 |
| | | | Burials | 1809-14 | |
| | | | Burials | 1809-36 | 1397 |
| | | | | | |
| 43 | SOUTHSEA | | | | |
| | Ebenezer Chapel | 1813 | Births | 1808-37 | 407 |
| | | | | | |
| 59 | WELLOW, ISLE OF WIGHT | | | | |
| | | 1804 | Births | 1810-37 | 1807 |

**HEREFORDSHIRE**

| | | | | | |
|---|---|---|---|---|---|
| 3 | GORSLEY or LINTON | | | | |
| | Particular Baptist | 1831 | Births | 1831-37 | 3571 |
| | | | | | |
| 5 | HEREFORD | 1828 | Births | 1831-37 | 2167 |

|  |  | Founded* |  |  | RG 4/ |
|---|---|---|---|---|---|

9    **KINGTON**
Lower Chapel,    1805    Births    1791-1837    1079
Particular Baptist

13    **LEOMINSTER**
Etnam Street Chapel    1656    Births    1747-1837 ⎫
   Burials    1702-1837 ⎬ 730

Etnam Street    Births    1785-92 ⎫
Particular Baptist    Births    1819 ⎬ 731
   Burials    1785-93 ⎭

17    **WESTON-UNDER-PENYARD**
Ryeford Chapel,    1662    Births    1787-91    2306
Particular Baptist    Births    1785-1837 ⎫
   Burials    1791-1836 ⎬ 2909

**HERTFORDSHIRE**

13    HEMEL HEMPSTED    1731    Births & ⎫
   Baptisms ⎬ 1785-1827 ⎫ 663
   Burials    1785-1824 ⎭
   Births    1822-36    664

\*    HEMEL HEMPSTEAD    Births    1824-37 ⎫
Pope's Lane    Burials    1837 ⎬ 665

19    HITCHIN    Births ⎫
Tilehouse Street    Baptisms ⎪
   Marriages ⎬ 1717-97 ⎫
   Burials ⎪ ⎬ 1808
   Burials    1785-92 ⎭
   Births ⎫
   Marriages ⎬ 1791-1837 ⎫
   Deaths ⎭ ⎬ 667
   Burials    1792-1836 ⎭

|  |  | Founded* |  |  | RG 4/ |
|---|---|---|---|---|---|
| 23 | KING'S WALDEN | | | | |
|  | Coleman's Green | 1785 | Births | 1807-37 | 669 |
| 27 | RICKMANSWORTH | | | | |
|  | formerly Independent | 1827 | Births | 1823-37 | 2113 |
| 30 | ST ALBANS | 1675 | Births | 1822-37 | 670 |
|  | Dagnall Lane | | Burials | 1822-37 | 1886 |
| 38 | WATFORD | 1703 | Births | 1785-1837 | } 674 |
|  |  | | Burials | 1794-1837 | |

\* Supplement between 14/3 and 15/1.

## HUNTINGDONSHIRE

| 1 | BLUNTISHAM | 1787 | Births & Baptisms } | 1788-1837 | } 626 |
|---|---|---|---|---|---|
|  |  | | Burials | 1787-1836 | |
|  |  | | Index | 1787-1837 | 3456 |
| 3 | KIMBOLTON | 1692 | Births | 1799-1836 | 3757 |
|  |  | | A bundle of Certificates corresponding with the above entries | | } 32 |
| 5 | NEEDINGWORTH-cum-HOLYWELL | | | | |
|  |  | 1767 | Births | 1824-37 | 677 |
| 8 | ST NEOTS | | | | |
|  | High Street | 1670 | Births | 1832-35 | } 3247 |
|  | Independent and Baptist | | Baptisms | 1802-22 | |
| 9 | SPALDWICK | before | Births | 1793-1837 | 3055 |
|  |  | 1737 | Certificates | | 22 |

| - | **ISLE OF WIGHT**: see **HAMPSHIRE** | | | | |

**KENT**

| - | BESSELL'S GREEN: see ORPINGTON, RG 4/1728 | | | | |

| 3 | BEXLEYHEATH | | | | |
|---|---|---|---|---|---|
| | Trinity [W.125] | 1827 | Burials | 1827-37 | 3891 |

| - | BOROUGH GREEN: see WROTHAM, RG 4/881 | | | | |

| 6 | BRABOURNE | 1818 | Births | 1817-37 | } |
|---|---|---|---|---|---|
| | Bethel Chapel | | Burials | 1819-37 | 679 |

| 11 | CANTERBURY | supposed | Births | 1780-1836 | } |
|----|---|---|---|---|---|
| | Blackfriars | upwards of 200 years | Burials | 1785-1836 | 751 |

| 16 | CHATHAM | 1700 | Births | 1700-1837 | 755 |
|----|---|---|---|---|---|
| | Heavyside Lane, now Hamond Hill | | Burials | 1785-1837 | 756 |

| 17 | CHATHAM | | | | |
|----|---|---|---|---|---|
| | Zion Chapel, Clover Street | | Burials | 1785-1837 | 916 |

| - | CHATHAM | | | | |
|----|---|---|---|---|---|
| | Providence Chapel, Brook | | Births | 1814-37 | |
| | | | [Unauthenticated Register RG 8/13] | | |

| 20 | CRANBROOK | 1700 | Births | 1682-1778 | } |
|----|---|---|---|---|---|
| | | | Burials | 1809-37 | 917 |

| | | Founded* | | | RG 4/ |
|---|---|---|---|---|---|

| | | **Founded*** | | | **RG 4/** |
|---|---|---|---|---|---|
| 35 | DOVER<br>St Mary's | 1643 | Births | 1730-1837 | 875 |
| - | DOVER<br>Pentside Chapel | | Births | 1809-37 | |
| | [Unauthenticated Register RG 8/15] | | | | |
| 40 | ERITH<br>Lessness Heath<br>Chapel [W91a] | 1799 | Births<br>Burials | 1807-32<br>1808-23 } | 876 |
| 42 | EYNSFORD<br>[W83] | 1796 | Births<br>Deaths & }<br>Burials } | 1799-1837<br><br>1805-37 } | 877 |
| 43 | EYTHORNE | 1600 | Births<br>Births<br>Births | 1723-93<br>1784-1829<br>1823-37 | 703A<br>1005<br>878 |
| 49 | FOLKESTONE | 1729 | Births | 1786-1836 | 940 |
| 47 | FOLKESTONE<br>Zion Chapel,<br>Fenchurch Street,<br>formerly Baptist,<br>but now Countess of Huntingdon's | 1786 | Births & }<br>Baptisms } | 1774-1836 | 1006 |
| 59 | HEADCORN | 1755 | Births<br>Deaths | 1731-1837<br>1780-1837 | 932 |
| - | LESSNESS HEATH: see ERITH, RG 4/876 | | | | |
| 67 | MAIDSTONE<br>King Street | 1797 | Births | 1800-36 | 935 |

| | | | | | | |
|---|---|---|---|---|---|---|
| 77 | ORPINGTON<br>Bessell's Green,<br>the Old Meeting House [W25] | 1715 or<br>1667 | Births<br>Burials | 1650-1837<br>1739-1837 | } | 1728 |

| | | | | | |
|---|---|---|---|---|---|
| - | ROLVENDEN | | Births &<br>Baptisms | 1796-1834 | |

A facsimile of the original register deposited at Dr Williams's Library, London, may be seen in the Public Record Office.

| | | | | | |
|---|---|---|---|---|---|
| 63 | ST PETERS<br>Isle of Thanet | 1797 | Births | 1789-1835 | 2309 |

| | | | | | |
|---|---|---|---|---|---|
| 83 | SANDHURST | 1731 | Births<br>Burials | 1785-1837<br>1786-1837 }| 1181 |

- SELLINDGE: see BRABOURNE, RG 4/679

- SELLING: see CANTERBURY, RG 4/751

| | | | | | |
|---|---|---|---|---|---|
| 87 | SEVENOAKS | 1820 | Births | 1820-34 | 1184 |

| | | | | | |
|---|---|---|---|---|---|
| 98 | TENTERDEN<br>Honey Lane | 1777 | Births | 1785-1837 | 1013 |

| | | | | | |
|---|---|---|---|---|---|
| 102 | TUNBRIDGE WELLS<br>Hanover Chapel | 1834 | Births | 1831-37 | 1757 |

| | | | | | |
|---|---|---|---|---|---|
| 112 | WOOLWICH<br>Enon Chapel [W57] | 1774 | Births | 1786-1836 | 1194 |

| | | | | | | |
|---|---|---|---|---|---|---|
| 110 | WOOLWICH<br>Queen Street Chapel<br>[W75] | 1788 | Births<br>Burials | 1781-1836<br>1821-36 | } | 1770 |

| | | | | | |
|---|---|---|---|---|---|
| 114 | WROTHAM<br>Borough Green | 1817 | Births | 1818-37 | 881 |

## LANCASHIRE

| | | | | | | |
|---|---|---|---|---|---|---|
| 1 | ACCRINGTON, OLD<br>Lower Chapel | 1760 | Births<br>Burials | 1782-1837<br>1786-1819 | } | 1995 |

| - | BACUP, Ebenezer Particular Baptist Chapel:<br>see ROSSENDALE, RG 4/999, 1731, 1614, 1000, 1001 |
|---|---|

| - | BACUP, Irwell Terrace Particular Baptist Chapel:<br>see ROSSENDALE, RG 4/1333 |
|---|---|

| | | | | | | |
|---|---|---|---|---|---|---|
| 15 | BLACKBURN<br>Islington | 1764 | Births<br>Burials | 1792-1837<br>1764-1837 | } | 1200 |
| 26 | BOLTON<br>Moor Lane<br>[formerly Scotch<br>Presbyterian] | 1821 | Births &<br>Baptisms }<br>Burials | 1793-1836<br>1813-15 } | | 1022 |
| 34 | BURNLEY<br>Sion Chapel,<br>Yorkshire Street | 1827 | Births | 1803-37 | | 2430 |
| 45 | BUTTERWORTH<br>Rochdale,<br>Ogden Chapel | 1780 | Births<br>Burials<br>Births<br>Burials<br>Births | 1782-1814<br>1784-1813 }<br>1813-25<br>1814-25 }<br>1820-37 | | 1029<br><br>2433<br>1118 |

| - | CLOUGHFOLD: see ROSSENDALE, RG 4/998 |
|---|---|

| | | | | | |
|---|---|---|---|---|---|
| 63 | COLNE | 1788 | Births | 1776-1836 | 1033 |
| 70 | ECCLES | 1831 | Births | 1831-37 | 2787 |

| | | Founded* | | | RG 4/ |
|---|---|---|---|---|---|
| 75 | EVERTON | | | | |
| | The Necropolis | | Burials | 1825-37 | 3121 |
| | Burial Ground (for all denominations) | | | | |
| | | | | | |
| 96 | INSKIP | 1817 | Births | 1812-37 | 829 |
| | | | | | |
| 102 | LANCASTER | 1809 | Births | 1798-1837 | |
| | Bryar Street | | Baptisms | 1809-37 } | 1475 |
| | Scotch Baptist | | | | |
| | | | | | |
| 113 | LIVERPOOL | 1783 | Births | 1783-1837 | |
| | Byrom Street | | Burials | 1783-1837 | 1479 |
| | | | | | |
| 128 | LIVERPOOL | | | | |
| | Lime Street Chapel, | 1800 | Births | 1818-37 | 969 |
| | formerly in Church Lane, Particular Baptist | | | | |
| | | | | | |
| 119 | LIVERPOOL | 1818 | Births & | | |
| | Great Cross Hall Street, | | Namings } | 1815-37 | 2557 |
| | Welsh Baptist | | | | |
| | | | | | |
| 131 | MANCHESTER | | | | |
| | St George's Road, | 1790 | Births | 1777-1836 | 2692 |
| | Oxford Street | | | | |
| | | | | | |
| 130 | MANCHESTER | | | | |
| | Oak Street, | 1824 | Births | 1819-36 | 2435 |
| | Green Street, General Baptist New Connexion | | | | |
| | | | | | |
| - | OGDEN: see BUTTERWORTH, RG 4/1029, 2433, 1118 | | | | |
| | | | | | |
| 159 | OLDHAM | | | | |
| | Manchester Street | 1815 | Births | 1816-37 | 981 |
| | | | | | |
| 180 | PRESTON | | | | |
| | Leeming Street Chapel | 1782 | Births | 1782-1836 | 986 |

| 190 | ROCHDALE | 1756 | Births | 1783-1836 | |
|  | Town Meadows Chapel, | | Burials | 1786-1818 | 1152 |
|  | now West Street Chapel, Particular Baptist | | | | |
| | | | | | |
| 192 | ROCHDALE | | | | |
|  | Hope Chapel, Hope St. | 1809 | Births & | | |
|  | Particular Baptist | | Baptisms } | 1805-37 | 1331 |
| | | | | | |
| 204 | ROSSENDALE, FOREST OF | | | | |
|  | Cloughfold | 1700 | Births | 1811-37 | 998 |
|  | Meeting House | | | | |
| | | | | | |
| 207A | ROSSENDALE, FOREST OF | | | | |
|  | Bacup, | 1720 | Births | 1759-88 } | |
|  | Ebenezer Particular | | Burials | 1783-88 } | 999 |
|  | Baptist Chapel | | Births | 1787-1816 } | |
|  | | | Burials | 1788-94 } | 1731 |
|  | | | Births | 1815-37 | 1614 |
|  | | | Burials | 1782-1806 | 1000 |
|  | | | Burials | 1812-37 | 1001 |
| | | | | | |
| 207B | ROSSENDALE, FOREST OF | | | | |
|  | Bacup, Irwell Terrace | 1821 | Births | 1790-1837 | 1333 |
|  | Particular Baptist Chapel | | | | |
| | | | | | |
| 209 | SABDEN, CLITHEROE | 1796 | Births | 1787-1819 } | |
|  | | | Burials | 1797-1837 } | 1122 |
|  | | | Births | 1806-37 | 135 |
|  | | | Births | 1833-39 | 2438 |
| | | | | | |
| 223 | STALEY BRIDGE | | | | |
|  | Ebenezer, Particular | 1813 | Births | 1807-37 | 2439 |
|  | Baptist Chapel | | | | |
| | | | | | |
| 224 | STALEY BRIDGE | | | | |
|  | Mount Pleasant Chapel | 1804 | Births | 1809-37 | 1164 |

| | | Founded* | | | RG 4/ |
|---|---|---|---|---|---|
| 231 | TOTTLEBANK | | | | |
| | Ulverston | 1669 | Burials | 1755-1837 | 3587 |

**LEICESTERSHIRE**

| | | Founded* | | | RG 4/ |
|---|---|---|---|---|---|
| 2 | ARNESBY | | | | |
| | formerly at KILBY | 1667 | Births | 1752-1836 | 1296 |
| 6 | CASTLE DONNINGTON | 1774 | Births & | | |
| | Band Gate Chapel | | Burials } | 1785-1835 | 2446 |
| 9 | FLECKNEY and SMEATON | | | | |
| | General Baptist Chapel | 1790 | Births | 1799-1836 | 1435 |
| 13 | HINCKLEY | 1763 | Births | 1776-1836 | 3187 |
| | Spring Gardens | Supplement-Births | | 1804-37 | 2321 |
| | General Baptist | | | | |
| 16 | KEGWORTH and DISEWORTH | | | | |
| | | 1752 | Births | 1785-1817 | 2447 |
| | | | Births | 1813-37 | 1440 |
| 19 | LEICESTER | | | | |
| | Dover Street | 1824 | Births | 1813-37 | 1442 |
| 20 | LEICESTER | | | | |
| | Friar Lane | 1688 | Births | 1802-37 | 1443 |
| | Meeting House | | | | |
| 21 | LEICESTER | | | | |
| | Upper Charles Street | 1831 | Burials | 1831-37 | 1125 |
| 26 | LONG WHATTON | | | | |
| | General Baptist | 1799 | Births | 1794-1837 | 1301 |
| | New Connexion | | | | |
| 28 | LOUGHBOROUGH | | | | |
| | Meeting House, | 1826 | Births | 1811-37 | 27 |
| | General Baptist | | Births | 1813-37 | 23 |

| 36 | MARKET HARBOROUGH General Baptist New Connexion | 1831 | Births | 1825-37 | 1458 |
|---|---|---|---|---|---|

| 45 | QUORNDON formerly with LOUGHBOROUGH | 1770 | Births Deaths & Burials } | 1760-1836 1786-1837 } | 1457 |
|---|---|---|---|---|---|

| 46 | ROTHLEY and SILEBY | 1800,1818 | Births | 1791-1836 | 1307 |
|---|---|---|---|---|---|

| 47 | SHEEPSHEAD | 1690 | Births Deaths } | 1754-1837 1785-94 } | 1456 |
|---|---|---|---|---|---|

| 49 | SYSTON | 1824 | Births | 1827-35 | 1455 |
|---|---|---|---|---|---|

| 51 | THURLASTON | 1813 | Births | 1798-1837 | 1695 |
|---|---|---|---|---|---|

| 55 | WOODHOUSE EAVES | 1796 | Births & Baptisms } Burials } | 1799-1837 1826-32 } | 1312 |
|---|---|---|---|---|---|

## LINCOLNSHIRE

| 7 | BOSTON High Street Chapel | 1650 | Births Births | 1809-37 1785-1830 | 2329 3130 |
|---|---|---|---|---|---|

| 6 | BOSTON High Street, Dissenters' Burial Ground | 1786 | Burials Burials Burials } | 1789-94 1829-37 1837-53 } | 24 25 |
|---|---|---|---|---|---|

| 15 | CARLTON-LE-MOORLAND | 1788 | Births | 1790-1837 | 1888 |
|---|---|---|---|---|---|

|  |  | **Founded*** |  |  | **RG 4/** |
|---|---|---|---|---|---|
| 17 | FLEET near Holbeach | 1709 | Births | 1709-98 | } |
|  |  |  | Burials | 1709-75 | } 1636A |
|  |  |  | Births | 1780-1826 | } |
|  |  |  | Burials | 1814-37 | } 2330 |
|  |  |  | Births | 1709-1837 | } |
|  |  |  | Burials | 1709-77 | } 1452 |
|  |  |  | Marriages | 1713-22 | } |
| 21 | GOSBERTON | 1650 | Births | 1703-1822 | } |
|  |  |  | Baptisms | 1703-27 | } |
|  |  |  | Burials | 1703-1802 | } 2829 |
|  |  |  | Marriages | 1717-55 | } |
|  |  |  | Births | 1819-36 | 1450 |
| 23 | GREAT GRIMSBY |  |  |  |  |
|  | Upper Burgess Street |  | Births | 1833-37 | 2331 |
| 31 | LINCOLN | 1781 | Births | 1756-1836 | } |
|  | Mint Lane Chapel |  | Burials | 1787-1826 | } 1449 |
| 32 | LINCOLN | 1701 | Births | 1816-36 | 1448 |
| 40A | LOUTH | 1802 | Births | 1810-36 | } |
|  |  |  | Burials | 1814-37 | } 368 |
| 44 | MONKSTHORP and BURGH |  | Births | 1786-94 | } |
|  |  |  | Burials | 1785-93 | } 2457 |
| 51 | SPALDING |  |  |  |  |
|  | Enon Chapel | 1688 | Births | 1819-37 | 367 |
| 52 | SPALDING |  |  |  |  |
|  | Ebenezer Chapel, | 1766 | Births | 1807-37 | 3957 |
|  | Love Lane |  |  |  |  |

|  |  | Founded* |  |  | RG 4/ |
|---|---|---|---|---|---|
| 57 | STAMFORD |  |  |  |  |
|  | Bath Row Chapel | 1828 | Births | 1831-36 | 4456 |
| 59 | SUTTERTON | 1804 | Births | 1823-36 | 369 |

**LONDON AND ENVIRONS (within a radius of four miles from St Paul's)**

| 5 | ARTILLERY STREET |  |  |  |  |
|---|---|---|---|---|---|
|  | Bishopsgate, | | Births | 1791-1811 | 4369 |
|  | Parliament Court Chapel [W77] |  |  |  |  |
| 24 | CAMBERWELL |  |  |  |  |
|  | Cold Harbour Lane | 1825 | Burials | 1825-36 | 4380 |
|  | [W126] |  |  |  |  |
| 33 | CHELSEA |  |  |  |  |
|  | Paradise Row [W108] | 1800 | Burials | 1800-36 | 4142 |
| 39 | CHRIST CHURCH |  |  |  |  |
|  | Church Street [W72] | 1785 | Births | 1772-1826 | 4522 |
| 46 | COMMERCIAL ROAD |  |  |  |  |
|  | Beulah Chapel, | about the | Births | 1787-1837 | 4268 |
|  | St George's East, | time of the |  |  |  |
|  | formerly | Protectorate |  |  |  |
|  | Church Lane, Whitechapel [W.11] |  |  |  |  |
| 52 | DEPTFORD |  |  |  |  |
|  | Church Street [W28] | 1802 | Burials | 1824-36 | 4184 |
| 59 | EAGLE STREET |  |  |  |  |
|  | Red Lion Square [W50] | 1737 | Births | 1770-1813 | 4235 |
| 61 | FETTER LANE |  |  |  |  |
|  | Elim Chapel [W71] | 1790 | Burials | 1791-1837 | 4391 |

| 83 | HENRIETTA STREET<br>Brunswick Square<br>[W109] | 1817 | Burials | 1828-37 | 4338 |
|----|----|----|----|----|----|
| 88 | HORSLEYDOWN<br>Goat Yard Passage,<br>then removed to<br>Carter Lane, Tooley Street<br>and in 1833 to New Park Street, Southwark [W44] | 1652 | Births<br>Marriages<br>Deaths | 1656-1712<br>1660-1700<br>1676-1712 } | 4188 |
| 106 | KEPPELL STREET<br>Russell Square<br>[W43] | 1713 | Births | 1788-1837 | 4275 |
| 123 | MAZE POND<br>Southwark [W34] | 1691 | Births<br>Burials | 1786-1830<br>1771-1837 | 4195<br>4516 |
| 130 | MILL YARD<br>Goodman's Fields<br>[W13] | 1600 | Burials<br>Burials | 1732-83<br>1783-1837 | 4505<br>4506 |
| 137 | OLD FORD<br>Bow [W73] | 1800 | Burials | 1814-37 | 4163 |
| 152 | PRESCOT STREET, LITTLE<br>Goodman's Fields,<br>at first meeting<br>in Wapping, then<br>in James Street,<br>Stepney [W3] | 1633 | Births | 1786-1803 | 4283 |
| 176 | ST LUKE'S<br>Great Mitchell Street<br>Meeting [W70] | 1783 | Births | 1787-1837 | 4174 |
| 186 | WALWORTH<br>East Street Chapel[W79] | 1787 | Burials<br>Burials | 1813-37<br>1837-52 | 4176<br>4514 |

| 192 | WILD STREET, LITTLE | | | | |
| | Lincoln's Inn Fields | 1691 | Burials | 1825-38 | 4364 |
| | [W40] | | Burials | 1835-37 | 4206 |

| 193 | WORSHIP STREET | | | | |
| | Finsbury [W36] | 1779 | Burials | 1787-1837 | 4515 |

**MIDDLESEX**

| 9 | HAMMERSMITH | | | | |
| | Trinity Chapel, | 1783 | Births | 1783-1837 | |
| | West End [W80] | | Burials | 1784-1814 | } 373 |
| | | | Burials | 1796-1837 | 2914 |

| 13 | HARROW-ON-THE-HILL | | | | |
| | [W99] | 1812 | Births | 1826-36 | 1239 |

**MONMOUTHSHIRE**

| 1 | ABERGAVENNY | | | | |
| | Frogmore Street | 1807 | Births | 1773-1837 | 1240 |

| 5 | ABERSTRWTH | | | | |
| | Hermon Chapel, | 1830 | Births | 1828-36 | 380 |
| | Nantyglo | | | | |

| 4 | ABERSYCHAN | 1828 | Births | 1830-37 | 2463 |

| 7 | BASSALEG | | | | |
| | Bethel Chapel | | Births | 1812-37 | 381 |
| 11 | CAERWENT | 1816 | Births | 1816-35 | |
| | | | Burials | 1817-35 | } 382 |

| 23 | MYNYDDYSLWYN | | | | |
| | Beulah Chapel | 1826 | Births | 1803-37 | 630 |

| | | | | | |
|---|---|---|---|---|---|
| - | NANTYGLO: see ABERSTRWTH, RG 4/380 | | | | |
| 29 | NEWPORT Commercial Street | 1829 | Births | 1832-37 | 632 |
| 37 | RAGLAND Ebenezer Chapel | 1818 | Births | 1820-37 | 1247 |
| 41 | RHYMNEY Iron Works, Penuel | 1821 | Births | 1806-36 | 634 |
| 50 | TROSNANT, PONTYPOOL | 1776 | Births | 1804-37 | 635 |

**NORFOLK**

| | | | | | |
|---|---|---|---|---|---|
| 1 | AYLSHAM | 1790 | Births Burials | 1791-1837 } 1791-1833 } | 637 |
| 3 | BACTON | 1822 | Births Burials | 1822-37 } 1824-36 } | 638 |
| 8 | BUXTON | 1796 | Births | 1794-1837 | 641 |
| 10 | DISS | 1789 | Births | 1819-36 | 1135 |
| - | DISS, ROYDON and other places in Norfolk and Suffolk | | Births & a few Marriages & Deaths | } 1780-1834 | |

[Unauthenticated Register RG 8/80]

| | | | | | |
|---|---|---|---|---|---|
| 13 | FAKENHAM | 1806 | Births | 1800-37 | 644 |
| 16 | FOULSHAM | 1824 | Births Burials | 1815-37 } 1823-25 } | 645 |

| | | Founded* | | | RG 4/ |
|---|---|---|---|---|---|
| 17 | FRAMLINGHAM | 1808 | Births | 1808-36 | 1136 |
| 18 | GREAT ELLINGHAM | 1699 | Burials | 1817-37 | 1254 |
| 22 | HACKFORD Reepham Chapel | 1821 | Births Deaths | 1805-33 1808-24 } | 646 |
| 24 | HIGHAM, NORWICH Rehoboth Chapel | 1824 | Births | 1796-1836 | 647 |
| 26 | INGHAM | | Births Burials | 1770-1837 1785-1821 } | 648 |
| - | KING'S LYNN: see LYNN REGIS, RG 4/1258, 1707 | | | | |
| 30 | LYNN REGIS Stepney Chapel, Broad Street | 1760 | Births Burials | 1789-1837 1843-57 | 1258 1707 |
| 36 | NEATISHEAD | 1811 | Births Burials | 1801-37 1812-37 } | 650 |
| 41 | NORWICH Priory Yard | 1660 | Births | 1821-36 | 652 |
| 49 | NORWICH St Mary's | 1698 | Births Burials Births Burials | 1761-1822 1789-1816 } 1822-37 1816-32 | 361 362 363 |
| 49A | NORWICH St Margaret's Chapel | 1778 | Births Burials | 1784-1838 1789-1856 } | 1785 |
| - | REEPHAM: see HACKFORD, RG 4/646 | | | | |

| | | Founded* | | | RG 4/ |
|---|---|---|---|---|---|
| - | ROYDON: see DISS, RG 4/1135 and RG 8/80 | | | | |
| 53 | SALEHOUSE | | | | |
| | Particular Baptist | 1801 | Births | 1802-37 | 2046 |
| 54 | SAXLINGHAM THORPE | | | | |
| | Particular Baptist | 1818 | Births | 1812-36 | 1137 |
| 55 | SHELFANGER | 1762 | Births | 1814-37 | 1138 |
| 65 | TITTLESHALL | | | | |
| | Particular Baptist | 1823 | Births | 1826-37 | 366 |

## NORTHAMPTONSHIRE

| | | Founded* | | | RG 4/ |
|---|---|---|---|---|---|
| 1 | ALDWINKLE | | | | |
| | St Peter's | 1820 | Births | 1797-1836 | 1889 |
| 4 | BLISWORTH | 1835 | Book of Certificates of Births } | 1794-1836 | 3360 |
| | | | Deaths | 1828-36 | 3601 |
| 7 | BRAUNSTON | 1788 | Burials | 1827-37 | 2474 |
| 10 | BURTON LATIMER | 1744 | Births | 1809-37 | 893 |
| 17 | EARL'S BARTON | 1793 | Births | 1770-1836 } | 896 |
| | | | Deaths | 1823-37 | |
| 20 | GRITTON | | | | |
| | Ebenezer Chapel | 1786 | Births | 1812-37 | 898 |
| 21 | HACKLETON | 1781 | Births | 1797-1836 | 890 |
| | | | Burials | 1803-36 | 1140 |

| | | Founded* | | | | RG 4/ |
|---|---|---|---|---|---|---|
| 24 | KETTERING<br>Silver Street | 1769 | Births<br>Burials | 1773-1837<br>1785-1837 | } | 136 |
| 27 | KING SUTTON | | Births &<br>Baptisms } | 1820-30 | | 2339 |
| 28 | KISLINGBURY | 1810 | Births | 1809-36 | | 3759 |
| 31 | MIDDLETON CHENEY<br>Great Chapel | | Births<br>Burials | 1785-1837<br>1789-93 | } | 1274 |
| 32 | MOULTON | 1680 | Certificates<br>of Births } | 1795-1836 | | 3361 |
| 34 | NORTHAMPTON<br>College Street | 1785 | Births<br>Burials | 1786-1837<br>1786-1837 | } | 902 |
| 43 | RINGSTEAD | 1714 | Births | 1792-1836 | | 907 |
| 44 | ROAD | 1720 | Births | 1816-37 | | 3960 |
| 47 | THRAPSTON | 1787 | Births<br>Burials | 1783-1837<br>1793-1837 | } | 909 |
| | | | Supplement-Births<br>& Baptisms } | 1808-31 | | 2918 |
| 48 | TOWCESTER | 1715 | Births | 1755-1836 | | 910 |
| 51 | WEEDON PINKNEY | 1695 | Births | 1780-1830 | | 1280 |
| 58 | WEST HADDON | 1821 | Births | 1815-37 | | 891 |

## NORTHUMBERLAND

| 12C | BERWICK-UPON-TWEED | | | | |
|---|---|---|---|---|---|
| | Calvinistic Baptist,<br>Walker Gate Lane | 1804 | Births | 1805-37 | 1576 |

| - | BROOMLEY: see DURHAM, ROWLEY, RG 4/3557 | | | | |
|---|---|---|---|---|---|

| 26 | NEWCASTLE-UPON-TYNE | | | | |
|---|---|---|---|---|---|
| | Tuthill Chapel | 1725 | Births | 1781-1837 | 2832 |

| 27 | NEWCASTLE-UPON-TYNE | | | | |
|---|---|---|---|---|---|
| | New Court Particular<br>Baptist Chapel,<br>Westgate Street | 1817 | Births | 1815-37 | 2833 |

| 41 | NORTH SHIELDS | | | | |
|---|---|---|---|---|---|
| | Particular Baptist<br>Baptist Chapel,<br>Stevenson Street | 1799 | Births<br>[indexed] | 1790-1837 | 2835 |

## NOTTINGHAMSHIRE

| 4 | BROUGHTON SULNEY, WIDMERPOOL and<br>HOSE in **LEICESTERSHIRE** | | | | |
|---|---|---|---|---|---|
| | General Baptist | 1800 | Births &<br>Baptisms } | 1802-34 | 2669 |

| 7 | EAST LEAKE and WIMESWOLD | | | | |
|---|---|---|---|---|---|
| | General Baptist | 1780 | Births | 1763-1824 | 2671 |
| | | | Births | 1775,<br>1799-1837 } | 2672 |

| 13 | KIRBY WOODHOUSE | 1746 | Births | 1748-1836 | 2485 |
|---|---|---|---|---|---|

| | | | | | |
|---|---|---|---|---|---|
| 16 | **MANSFIELD**<br>Stockwell Gate Chapel | 1800 | Births | 1806-37 | 1584 |
| 27 | **NOTTINGHAM**<br>George Street before 1742<br>Chapel, removed<br>from Friar Lane Chapel in 1815 | | Births<br>Burials | 1742-1836 }<br>1785-1837 } | 1351 |
| 28 | **NOTTINGHAM**<br>Broad Street | 1775 | Births<br>Births | 1784-1830<br>1801-37 | 1589<br>2676 |
| 26 | **NOTTINGHAM**<br>Stoney Street<br>see also OLD BASFORD, RG 4/2677 | 1799 | Births | 1809-37 | 2675 |
| 29 | **NOTTINGHAM**<br>Bethesda Meeting,<br>Barker Gate,<br>Paradise Place | 1828 | Births | 1806-37 | 1718 |
| 37 | **OLD BASFORD**<br>and Stoney Street<br>Chapel, Nottingham | | Births | 1801-37 | 2677 |
| 44 | **SUTTON BONNINGTON**<br>General Baptist<br>near Loughborough | 1798 | Births | 1785-1837 | 1782 |
| 46 | **SUTTON-IN-ASHFIELD** | 1760 | Births | 1760-1810 | 3603 |

**OXFORDSHIRE**

| | | | | | |
|---|---|---|---|---|---|
| 7 | **BURFORD**<br>Witney Street | 1700 | Births<br>Deaths &<br>Burials } | 1809-35<br>1830-36 | } 2051 |

|  |  | **Founded*** |  |  | **RG 4/** |
|---|---|---|---|---|---|
| 9 | CHIPPING NORTON | 1662 | Births | 1767-1830 | 3763 |
|  |  |  | Births | 1767-1830 | 2845 |
|  |  |  |  |  |  |
| 11 | COATE | 1664 | Births | 1647-1836 |  |
|  | parish of Bampton |  | Burials | 1657-1837 | 140 |
|  |  |  |  |  |  |
| 20 | SYDENHAM | 1821 | Births & |  |  |
|  |  |  | Deaths } | 1821-36 | 2793 |
|  |  |  |  |  |  |
| 21 | THAME | 1825 | Births | 1826-37 | 1601 |
|  |  |  |  |  |  |
| 23 | WITNEY | 1700 | Births & |  |  |
|  | Independent |  | Baptisms } | 1799-1819 | 2794 |
|  | and Baptist |  | Births & |  |  |
|  |  |  | Baptisms } | 1822-36 | 1602 |

## RUTLANDSHIRE

| 2 | MOORCOTT and BARROWDEN |  |  |  |  |
|---|---|---|---|---|---|
|  |  | 1710 & 1806 | Births | 1769-1837 | 1811 |
| 3 | OAKHAM | 1772 | Births | 1766-1837 |  |
|  |  |  | Burials | 1786-1827 } | 1603 |

## SHROPSHIRE

| 3 | BRIDGNORTH | 1705 | Births & |  |  |
|---|---|---|---|---|---|
|  | Castle Street Chapel |  | Deaths } | 1779-1836 | 1605 |
|  |  |  |  |  |  |
| 5 | BROSELEY |  |  |  |  |
|  | Birch Meadow Chapel | 1800 | Births | 1794-1837 | 1892 |
|  |  |  |  |  |  |
| 8 | CHIRBURY | 1829 | Births | 1827-35 | 2796 |
|  |  |  |  |  |  |
| 30 | PONTESBURY | 1826 | Births | 1828-37 | 1893 |

| 34 | SHIFNAL | | | | | |
|----|---------|------|--------|-----------|------|
| | Aston Street | 1780 | Births | 1811-36 | 1817 |

| 36 | SHREWSBURY | 1620 | Births | 1766-1825 | 1819 |
|----|------------|------|--------|-----------|------|
| | Claremont Street | | Births | 1813-36 | 2798 |
| | Meeting House | | | | |

| 45 | WEM | | | | |
|----|-----|------|--------|---------|------|
| | Cripple Street | 1813 | Births | 1823-36 | 1821 |

**SOMERSETSHIRE**

| 5 | BATH | 1720 | Births | 1763-89 | 3195 |
|---|------|------|--------|---------|------|
| | Somerset Street | | Births | 1784-1836 | |
| | | | Burials | 1785-1837 | } 1790 |

| 19 | BRISTOL | | Burials | 1679-1746 | 3765 |
|----|---------|--|---------|-----------|------|
| | Broad Mead | | Burials | 1746-91 | 2871 |
| | | | Burials | 1789-1803 | 1826 |
| | | | Burials | 1804-36 | 1827 |
| | | | Burials | 1836-37 | 1828 |
| | | | Burials | 1756-1827 | 1829 |
| | | | Burials | 1825-34 | 2923 |
| | | | Births | 1787-1817 | 2697 |
| | | | Births | 1813-37 | 1358 |

| 19A | BRISTOL | | | | |
|-----|---------|--|---------|---------|------|
| | King Street | | Burials | 1827-55 | 2698 |

| 31 | CHARD | 1652 | Births | 1786-94 | 34 |
|----|-------|------|--------|---------|------|
| | | | Births | 1807-37 | |
| | | | Burials | 1836-37 | } 2689 |

| 34 | CREWKERNE | | | | |
|----|-----------|------|--------|---------|------|
| | North Street Chapel | 1820 | Births | 1831-37 | 2699 |

|  |  | Founded* |  |  | RG 4/ |
|---|---|---|---|---|---|
| 44 | FROME | 1689 | Births | 1801-37 | 3261 |
|  | Badcox Lane |  | Burials | 1785-1827 | 1550 |
|  | Meeting House |  | Burials | 1832-37 | 3264 |
| 45 | FROME | 1707 | Births | 1785-95 | } 1551 |
|  | Sheppard's Barton |  | Burials | 1792-95 |  |
|  | Meeting House |  | Births | 1802-36 | 3262 |
|  |  |  | Burials | 1764-1826 | 2925 |
|  |  |  | Burials | 1750-1837 | *3263 |

*RG 4/3263 includes copies of entries for Meeting House Burial Ground and a few entries relating to St Catherine Hill Burial Ground, 1750-1824, compiled from Sexton's book.

| 62 | PAULTON |  |  |  |  |
|---|---|---|---|---|---|
|  | near Bath | 1690 | Births | 1785-1836 | } 1733 |
|  |  |  | Burials | 1827-36 |  |
| 65 | ROWBERROW | 1814 | Births | 1816-37 | 1559 |
| 74 | STOGUMBER | 1726 | Births | 1810-36 | 1565 |
| 75 | STREET | 1814 | Births | 1814-37 | } 1422 |
|  |  | closed 1837 | Burials | -1837 |  |
| 78 | TAUNTON | 1815 | Births | 1782-1837 | } 3219 |
|  | Silver Street |  | Burials | 1823-36 |  |
| 76 | TAUNTON |  |  |  |  |
|  | Octagon Chapel, | 1816 | Births | 1816-26 | 1566 |
|  | Middle Street |  |  |  |  |
| 83 | WELLINGTON | 1750 | Births | 1784-96 | } 1750 |
|  |  |  | Burials | 1785-93 |  |
|  |  |  | Births | 1781-1837 | } 1736 |
|  |  |  | Burials | 1809-30 |  |

| 87 | WELLS | | | | |
|---|---|---|---|---|---|
| | Ebenezer Chapel | 1814 | Births | 1814-35 | 2935 |

| 94 | YEOVIL | | | | |
|---|---|---|---|---|---|
| | South Street Chapel | 1688 | Births | 1810-36 | 1737 |

**STAFFORDSHIRE**

| - | BRETTELL LANE: see KINGSWINFORD, RG 4/3296 |
|---|---|

| 6 | BURSLEM | | Births | 1791-1837 | 3856 |
|---|---|---|---|---|---|

| 10 | BURTON-UPON-TRENT | | | | |
|---|---|---|---|---|---|
| | Cat Street Chapel   before 1800 | | Births | 1793-1836 | 2129 |

| 13 | BURTON EXTRA | | | | |
|---|---|---|---|---|---|
| | Burton-upon-Trent | 1824 | Births | 1821-37 | 3363 |

| 19 | CLENT | | | | |
|---|---|---|---|---|---|
| | Holy Cross | 1802 | Births | 1807-36 | 2718 |

| 20 | COPPICE, COSELEY | 1804 | Births & Namings } | 1794-1819 | 1868 |
|---|---|---|---|---|---|
| | | | Births | 1819-37 | 2719 |

| 22 | COSELEY | | | | |
|---|---|---|---|---|---|
| | Darkhouse Chapel, parish of Sedgley | 1786 | Births | 1791-1837 | 2803 |

| 21 | COSELEY | 1809 | Births & Namings } | 1809-37 | 3295 |
|---|---|---|---|---|---|
| | Providence Chapel, parish of Sedgley | | | | |

| 29 | KINGSWINFORD | | | | |
|---|---|---|---|---|---|
| | Brettell Lane | 1798 | Births | 1778-1836 | 3296 |

|  |  |  | **Founded*** |  |  | **RG 4/** |
|---|---|---|---|---|---|---|
| 68 | WOLVERHAMPTON | | | | | |
|  | Walsall Street | 1829 | Births & Namings } | 1832-37 | | 1876 |
| | **SUFFOLK** | | | | | |
| 1 | ALDRINGHAM | 1812 | Births | 1812-37 | | 1741 |
| 2 | BARDWELL | 1824 | Births | 1820-37 | | 2823 |
| 5 | BECCLES | 1805 | Burials | 1828-37 | | 1833 |
| 12 | CHELMONDISTON | 1824 | Births | 1810-34 } | | 1835 |
|  |  |  | Burials | 1831-34 | | |
|  |  |  | Birth Certificates } | 1831-37 | | 3924 |
| 14 | CLARE | 1803 | Deaths | 1822-35 | | 2127 |
| 19 | EYE | 1810 | Births | 1805-36 } | } | 3196 |
|  |  |  | Deaths & Burials } | 1812-34 | | |
| 22 | FRAMSDEN | 1835 | Births | 1831-37 | | 2355 |
| 24 | GRUNDISBURGH | | Births | 1804-35 | | 16 |
|  |  |  | Births | 1816-37 | | 17 |
| 25 | HADLEIGH | | | | | |
|  | George Street | 1820 | Births | 1821-37 | | 1841 |
| 30 | IPSWICH | 1758 | Births | 1785-1837 | | 1846 |
|  | Stoke Green | | Burials | 1829-37 | | 1847 |
|  |  |  | Burials | 1850-55 | | 2824 |
| 32 | IPSWICH | | | | | |
|  | Dairy Lane | 1829 | Births | 1810-37 | | 1850 |

| | | Founded* | | | RG 4/ |
|---|---|---|---|---|---|
| 42 | LOWESTOFT | | | | |
| | High Street Chapel | 1812 | Births | 1812-28 | 1429 |
| 43 | MILDENHALL | | | | |
| | West Row | 1813 | Births | 1802-37 | 2705 |
| 49 | OTLEY | 1800 | Births | 1800-36 | 1856 |
| 55 | STRADBROKE | 1814 | Births | 1814-36 | 2825 |
| 58 | WALSHAM-LE-WILLOWS | 1822 | Births | 1811-37 | 2804 |
| 59 | WALTON | 1808 | Births | 1807-37 | 2709 |

Unauthenticated Register RG 8/66 lists Baptist burials at various places in Suffolk, 1780-1834. It also contains a few entries of deaths and a marriage during the above period, and may be seen in the Public Record Office at press No. 69.

**SURREY**

| | | Founded* | | | RG 4/ |
|---|---|---|---|---|---|
| 2 | BETCHWORTH | | | | |
| | Brockham Chapel | 1785 | Births | 1785-1836 | 3925 |
| 11 | CHOBHAM | | | | |
| | West End Chapel | 1796 | Births | 1810-36 | 1742 |
| 13 | CLAPHAM | | | | |
| | Particular Baptist Chapel [W76] | 1777 | Births | 1781-1835 | 3059 |
| 30 | KINGSTON-UPON-THAMES | | | | |
| | Particular Baptist | 1790 | Births | 1783-1807 | 2126 |
| | Chapel, Brick Lane | | Births | 1802-37 | 3424 |
| | [W78] | Supplement- | Births | 1837 | 2938 |
| | | | Deaths | 1799-1836 | 3425 |

| | | Founded* | | | RG 4/ |
|---|---|---|---|---|---|
| 45 | WANDSWORTH | 1821 | Births | 1816-34 | 1901 |
| | Particular Baptist | | Burials | 1825-36 | 2216 |
| | Bridge Field Meeting [W122] | | | | |

## SUSSEX

| | | Founded* | | | RG 4/ |
|---|---|---|---|---|---|
| 4 | BILLINGSHURST | | | | |
| | General Baptist Chapel | | Burials | 1821-36 | 2989 |
| 7 | BRIGHTON | 1785 | Births | 1775-1835 ⎫ | |
| | Salem Chapel, | | Burials | 1790-1834 ⎬ | 2712 |
| | Bond Street | | Births | 1835-37 | 2940 |
| 22 | DITCHLING | | | | |
| | General Baptist | before 1741 | Baptisms | 1811-33 | 1796 |
| | Meeting House | | Burials | 1821-37 | 1797 |
| 25 | HAILSHAM | 1794 | Births & Namings ⎫⎬ | 1794-1837 | 2622 |
| 32 | HORSHAM | 1700 | Births & Baptisms ⎫⎬ | 1688, 1706-1836 ⎫ | |
| | General Baptist | | Burials | 1771-1836 ⎬ | 2729 |
| | Chapel | | Burials | 1721-68 | 2062 |
| 36 | LEWES | 1776 | Births | 1788-1837 | 2966 |
| 45 | ROTHERFIELD | 1774 | Births | 1828-36 ⎫ | |
| | | | Deaths | 1784-1829 ⎬ | 3631 |
| 46 | RYE | 1750 | Births | 1769-83 ⎫ | |
| | | | Burials | 1768-1808 ⎬ | 3365 |
| | | | Births | 1786-1837 ⎫ | |
| | | | Deaths | 1785-1836 ⎬ | 2968 |

- SHOVERS GREEN: see WADHURST, RG 4/3366, 2366

| | | Founded* | | | RG 4/ |
|---|---|---|---|---|---|
| 50 | UCKFIELD | | | | |
| | Rock Hall | 1787 | Births | 1783-1835 | } 2969 |
| | Meeting House | | Burials | 1792-1837 | |
| | | | | | |
| 51 | WADHURST | 1815 | Births & | | |
| | Shovers Green | | Baptisms } | 1818-37 | 3366 |
| | | | Burials | 1832-35 | 2366 |
| | | | | | |
| 54 | WIVELSFIELD | 1763 | Births & | | |
| | | | Baptisms } | 1790-1837 | } 2970 |
| | | | Burials | 1790-1837 | |

## WARWICKSHIRE

| | | | | | |
|---|---|---|---|---|---|
| - | ALCESTER: see WORCESTERSHIRE, FECKENHAM, RG 4/2016 | | | | |
| | | | | | |
| 11 | BIRMINGHAM | 1737 | Births | 1785-1801 | 2972 |
| | Cannon Street | | Births | 1798-1814 | 3636 |
| | | | Births | 1782-1835 | 2973 |
| | | | Births | 1799-1837 | 3114 |
| | | Supplement-Births | | 1817-37 | 3116 |
| | | | Burials | 1786-94 | 2972 |
| | | | Burials | 1799-1837 | 3115 |
| | | | | | |
| 10 | BIRMINGHAM | 1785 | Births | 1775-1837 | } 3113 |
| | Bond Street | | Burials | 1794-1837 | |
| | | | | | |
| 8 | BIRMINGHAM | 1786 | Births | 1786-1808 | 4109 |
| | Lombard Street | | Births | 1813-36 | 1903 |
| | | | | | |
| 12 | BIRMINGHAM | | | | |
| | Zion Chapel, | 1796 | Births | 1821-37 | 3117 |
| | New Hall Street | | | | |
| | | | | | |
| 28 | COVENTRY | 1773 | Births | 1769-1837 | } 2981 |
| | Longford Chapel | | Burials | 1801-37 | |

|  |  | Founded* |  |  | RG 4/ |
|---|---|---|---|---|---|
| 29 | COVENTRY Cow Lane, formerly Jordan Well | 1793 | Births [indexed] | 1761-1836 | 2982 |
| 32 | COVENTRY General Baptist, Whitefriars' Lane | 1825 | Births | 1826-37 | 2627 |
| 33 | DRAYCOTT parish of Bourton | 1811 | Births & Namings } | 1812-37 | 3202 |
| 37 | HENLEY-IN-ARDEN | 1700 | Births | 1791-1830 | 4481 |
| 45 | MONK'S KIRBY | 1817 | Births | 1805-37 | 1712 |
| 55 | WOLSTEN | 1810 | Births | 1811-37 | 2956 |
|  | **WESTMORLAND** | [NONE] |  |  |  |
|  | **WILTSHIRE** |  |  |  |  |
| 1 | ALLINGTON parish of All Cannings | 1829 | Births | 1826-37 | 2984 |
| 13 | CHIPPENHAM | 1804 | Births | 1789-1837 | 2987 |
| 17 | DEVIZES | 16th century | Births Deaths & Burials } | 1772-1837 1780-1836 | } 2230 |
| 22 | DOWNTON South Lane Chapel | 1738 | Births Burials | 1800-37 1794-1836 | } 2013 |
| 24 | EAST KNOYLE and SEMLEY | 1824 | Births | 1821-37 | 4486 |

|       |                                      | Founded* |         |           | RG 4/ |
|-------|--------------------------------------|----------|---------|-----------|-------|
| 32    | LUDGERSHALL                          | 1816     | Births  | 1817-36   | 2131  |
|       |                                      |          | Births  | 1833-37   |       |
|       |                                      |          | Burials | 1826-35   | 2235  |
| 37    | MALMESBURY<br>Abbey Row              |          | Births  | 1794-1837 | 2238  |
| 42    | MELKSHAM                             | 1714     | Births  | 1794-1837 |       |
|       |                                      |          | Burials | 1794-1837 | 3043  |
| 45    | NETHERAVON                           |          | Births  | 1814-37   | 2241  |
| 46    | NETTLETON                            | 1826     | Births  | 1827-36   |       |
|       |                                      |          | Burials | 1826-32   | 2132  |
| 48    | NORTH BRADLEY                        | 1779     | Births  | 1790-1836 | 3045  |
|       |                                      |          | Burials | 1779-1837 | 2242  |
| 51    | SALISBURY<br>Brown Street            | 1688     | Births  | 1785-87   |       |
|       |                                      |          | Births  | 1788-91   | 2064  |
|       |                                      |          | Births  | 1763-1837 |       |
|       |                                      |          | Burials | 1792-1836 | 1433  |
| 58    | TROWBRIDGE<br>Back Street            | 1737     | Burials | 1822-37   | 3047  |
| 61    | TROWBRIDGE<br>Conigree Chapel        | 1660     | Births  | 1816-37   | 2958  |
| 64    | WARMINSTER<br>Ebenezer Chapel,<br>North Row | 1812 | Burials | 1812-36   | 2740  |

## WORCESTERSHIRE

| | | *Founded | | | RG 4/ |
|---|---|---|---|---|---|
| - | ASTWOOD: see FECKENHAM, RG 4/2016 | | | | |
| 1 | BEWDLEY | 1649 | Births | 1776-1836 | 2066 |
| | | | Deaths & | 1758-1836 | |
| | | | Burials | 1758-1836 | |
| 5 | BROMSGROVE Worcester Street, Independent and Baptist | 1787 | Births & Baptisms | 1785-1804 | 2734 |
| | | | Births | 1804-36 | |
| 7 | BROMSGROVE Little Cat's Hill | 1820 | Births Baptisms Deaths Burials | 1830-37 | 2136 |
| 9 | CRADLEY | 1801 | Births & Dedications | 1794-1836 | 3371 |
| | | | Burials | 1805-37 | |
| 12 | DUDLEY New Street Chapel | 1766 | Births | 1816-37 | 2735 |
| | | | Deaths | 1814-37 | |
| 18 | FECKENHAM, Astwood Chapel, and Alcester in **WARWICKSHIRE** | 1793 | Births | 1788-1837 | |
| | | | Deaths | 1801-06 | 2016 |
| | | | Burials | 1800-37 | 2067 |
| 22 | KIDDERMINSTER Union Street Chapel | 1813 | Births | 1814-37 | 2739 |
| 30 | SHIPSTON-UPON-STOUR | 1778 | Births | 1783-1836 | 3375 |
| 34 | TENBURY Cross Street Chapel | 1816 | Births | 1820-36 | 2068 |

| 37 | WORCESTER Silver Street Chapel | 1712 | Births | 1793-1837 | 1908 |
|---|---|---|---|---|---|

## YORKSHIRE

| 5 | ALMONDBURY Broadlands Chapel | 1816 | Births | 1809-38 | 3377 |
|---|---|---|---|---|---|

| 22 | BARNOLDSWICK Bridge Chapel | 1650 | Births Burials | 1785-1837 1786-1834 | } 3930 |
|---|---|---|---|---|---|

| 23 | BEDALE Ebenezer Chapel | 1793 | Births Baptisms Births | 1785-1827 1793-1822 1808-27 | } 3381 3382 |
|---|---|---|---|---|---|

| 26 | BEVERLEY Walker Gate Chapel | 1791 | Births | 1787-1836 | 1909 |
|---|---|---|---|---|---|

| 33 | BISHOP BURTON | 1770 | Births Burials | 1755-1836 1776-94 | } 3223 |
|---|---|---|---|---|---|

| - | BOROUGHBRIDGE: see DISHFORTH and BOROUGHBRIDGE, RG 4/2997 | | | | |
|---|---|---|---|---|---|

| 40 | BRADFORD Westgate Chapel | 1753 Supplement-Births | Births | 1784-1837 1812-37 | 1910 4433 |
|---|---|---|---|---|---|

| 38 | BRADFORD Sion Chapel, Bridge Street | 1824 Supplement-Births | Births | 1814-37 1814-37 | 2991 3385 |
|---|---|---|---|---|---|

| - | BRADFORD: for other Baptist churches, see CLAYTON, RG 4/2993, 3025, 3026, 3027, 3516, 3436 and HEATON, RG 4/2142 | | | | |
|---|---|---|---|---|---|

|    |                | Founded* |                |             | RG 4/ |
|----|----------------|----------|----------------|-------------|-------|
| 45 | BRAMLEY        | 1779     | Births         | 1783-1803   | 3142  |
|    | the Lane Chapel |         | Births         | 1799, 1803-18 | 3141 |
|    |                |          | Births & Namings | 1818-24   | 1714  |
|    |                |          | Births         | 1824-37     | 2810  |
|    |                |          | Deaths         | 1823-37     | 3321  |
| 48 | BRIDLINGTON    | 1698     | Births         | 1698-1783   | 3019  |
|    |                |          | Marriages      | 1700-43     |       |
|    |                |          | Burials        | 1700-47     |       |
|    |                |          | Births         | 1783-1836   | 3143  |
|    |                |          | Burials        | 1783-1837   |       |
| 63 | CLAYTON        |          |                |             |       |
|    | parish of Bradford | 1830 | Births         | 1782, 1801-37 | 2993 |
| 64 | CLAYTON        | 1773     | Births         | 1748-1829   | 3025  |
|    | Queen's Head Chapel, |    | Burials        | 1788-94     |       |
|    | parish of Bradford |      | Burials        | 1831-37     |       |
|    |                |          | Births         | 1786-1837   | 3026  |
|    |                |          | Births         | 1766-1837   | 3027  |
|    |                |          | Births         | 1776-1837   | 3516  |
| 65 | CLAYTON        |          |                |             |       |
|    | West Chapel    | 1821     | Births         | 1818-37     | 3436  |
| 72 | CRIGGLESTONE   | 1822     | Births & Burials | 1822-37   | 4480  |
|    | near Wakefield |          |                |             |       |
| 85 | DISHFORTH and BOROUGHBRIDGE | | |         |       |
|    | Dishforth and  | 1816     | Births         | 1819-37     | 2997  |
|    | Langforth Chapels |       |                |             |       |
| 92 | EARBY          | 1819     | Births         | 1802-37     | 1913  |

71

| 107 | FARSLEY Rehoboth Chapel | 1777 | Births Burials | 1779-1837 1785-1837 } | 3160 |
|---|---|---|---|---|---|
| 112 | GILDERSOME Parish of Batley or rather earlier | 1717 | Births & Baptisms [with Index] } | 1799-1837 | 3006 |
| 114 | GOLCAR | 1836 | Births & Namings } Burials | 1833-38 1835-37 } | 2812 |
| 121 | GREAT DRIFFIELD | 1788 | Births | 1796-1835 | 3008 |
| 131 | HALIFAX Pellon Lane Chapel | 1763 | Births Deaths & Burials } | 1779-1837 1785-1837 | 3165 3166 |

- HALIFAX: for other Baptist churches, see RISHWORTH, RG 4/2752, 2753 and WADSWORTH, RG 4/2775, 2776

- HALLIFIELD: see HELLIFIELD RG 4/3171

| 149 | HEATON Bethel, or Swaine Boyd Lane Bottom Chapel, parish of Bradford | 1824 | Births | 1798, 1807-37 } | 2142 |
|---|---|---|---|---|---|

- HEBDEN BRIDGE: see WADSWORTH, Birchcliff, RG 4/2775, 2776

| 141 | HELLIFIELD and LONG PRESTON | 1807 | Births & Baptisms } | 1803-37 | 3171 |
|---|---|---|---|---|---|
| 150 | HEPTONSTALL Ebenezer Chapel | 1777 | Births Burials | 1745-1837 1785-94 } | 3176 |

|  |  | Founded* |  |  | RG 4/ |
|---|---|---|---|---|---|
| 51 | HEPTONSTALL SLACK | 1807 | Births | 1789-1837 | 3014 |
|  | Mount Zion Chapel |  | Burials | 1808-37 | 2642 |
| 64 | HORSFORTH |  |  |  |  |
|  | near Leeds, | 1801 | Births | 1800-35 | 3471 |
|  | Zion Chapel |  | Births | 1800-37 | 3136 |
| 72 | HUDDERSFIELD |  |  |  |  |
|  | Pole Moor Chapel | 1788 | Births | 1831-37 | 2814 |
| 73 | HUDDERSFIELD |  |  |  |  |
|  | Lockwood Chapel | 1795 | Births | 1792-1837 | 2744 |

HUDDERSFIELD: see also SALENDINE NOOK, RG 4/2748, 2749

| 80 | HULL | 1796 | Births | 1774, | ⎫ |  |
|---|---|---|---|---|---|---|
|  | George Street Chapel |  |  | 1794-1837 | ⎬ | 3204 |
| 83 | HULL |  |  |  |  |  |
|  | Unitarian Baptist |  | Births | 1801-12 |  | 4483 |
| 92 | HUNMANBY | 1817 | Births | 1786-1836 | ⎫ |  |
|  |  |  | Deaths & ⎱ |  | ⎬ | 3227 |
|  |  |  | Burials ⎰ | 1819-36 | ⎭ |  |
| 96 | IDLE | 1810 | Burials | 1810-37 |  | 79 |
| 01 | KEIGHLEY | 1811 | Births | 1791-1837 | ⎱ |  |
|  | Bethel Chapel |  | Burials | 1830-36 | ⎰ | 3393 |
| 06 | KILDWICK | 1711 | Births | 1768, | ⎫ |  |
|  | Sutton Chapel |  |  | 1785-1837 | ⎬ | 1915 |
|  |  |  | Burials | 1785-94 | ⎭ |  |
| 07 | KILHAM | 1820 | Births | 1821-36 |  | 3233 |

KINGSTON-UPON-HULL: see HULL, RG 4/3204, 4483

| 224 | LEEDS | | | | |
|---|---|---|---|---|---|
| | South Parade,<br>formerly The Old Baptist Chapel | 1779 | Births | 1785-1837 | 3761 |

| 234A | LEEDS | | | |
|---|---|---|---|---|
| | Ebenezer Chapel | Births | 1782-97 | } 3432 |
| | | Burials | 1786-94 | |

-     LOCKWOOD: see HUDDERSFIELD, Lockwood Chapel, RG 4/2744

-     LONG PRESTON: see HELLIFIELD RG 4/3171

| 257 | MASBOROUGH | | Births | 1789-1835 | 3406 |
|---|---|---|---|---|---|

| 264 | MILLWOOD | | | | |
|---|---|---|---|---|---|
| | Rehoboth Chapel | 1808 | Births | 1699-1832 | 2649 |

| 265 | MIRFIELD<br>near Dewsbury | 1825 | Births<br>Burials | 1825-37<br>1833-37 | } 1918 |
|---|---|---|---|---|---|
| 276 | NEW MALTON | | | | |
| | Salem Chapel | 1824 | Births | 1829-36 | 2658 |

-     POLE MOOR: see HUDDERSFIELD, Pole Moor Chapel, RG 4/2814

| 301 | QUARMBY-cum-LINDLEY | | | | |
|---|---|---|---|---|---|
| | Salendine Nook<br>Meeting House,<br>parish of Huddersfield | 1743 | Births &<br>Dedications }<br>Burials | 1783-1823<br>1783-94,<br>1809 | } 2748 |
| | | | Births | 1820-37 | 2749 |

| 302 | RAWDEN | 1715 | Births | 1755-1808 | | 37 |
|-----|--------|------|--------|-----------|---|-----|
| | Brixstone Chapel | | Births | 1783-92 | ⎫ | |
| | | | Burials | 1783-91 | ⎬ | 2080 |
| | | | Births | 1780-1817 | ⎫ | |
| | | | Burials | 1793-1818 | ⎬ | 2081 |
| | | | Births | 1803-37 | ⎫ | |
| | | | Burials | 1837 | ⎬ | 2815 |
| | | | | | | |
| 313 | RISHWORTH | | | | | |
| | Roadside Chapel, | 1802 | Births | 1802-24 | | 2752 |
| | parish of Halifax | | Births | 1824-37 | | 2753 |

- SALENDINE NOOK: see QUARMBY-cum-LINDLEY, RG 4/2748, 2749

| 322 | SCARBOROUGH | | | | | |
|-----|-------------|------|--------|-----------|---|------|
| | Ebenezer | 1771 | Births | 1767-1834 | ⎫ | |
| | Meeting House | | Burials | 1776-1835 | ⎬ | 3685 |
| | | | | | | |
| 353 | SKIDBY | | | | | |
| | Tabernacle | 1826 | Births | 1824-36 | | 2764 |
| | | | | | | |
| 391 | THURLSTONE | 1828 | Births | 1817-37 | | 2614 |
| | | | | | | |
| 394 | WADSWORTH | 1764 | Births | 1785-1812 | | 2775 |
| | Birchcliff, | | Births | 1797-1837 | ⎫ | |
| | parish of Halifax | | Burials | 1816-37 | ⎬ | 2776 |
| | | | | | | |
| 420 | YORK | | | | | |
| | New Jubbergate, | 1799 | Births | 1779-1835 | | 3518 |
| | formerly College | | | | | |
| | Street, then | | | | | |
| | Peasholme Green | | | | | |

# WALES

## ANGLESEA

| | | | | | |
|---|---|---|---|---|---|
| 9 | BRIENSIENCYN [=BRYNSIENCYN]<br>and PENYCARNEDDI | | | | |
| | The Tabernacle,<br>Llanidan | 1810 | Births | 1811-37 | 3547 |
| 16 | LLANERCHYMEDD | | | | |
| | Tabernacle,<br>parish of Amlwch | 1817 | Births | 1805-28 | 3937 |
| 57 | LLANRHYDDLAD | | | | |
| | Rhydwyn Chapel | 1802 | Births | 1789-1836 | 3791 |
| 51 | PENYMYNYDD,<br>PENYCARNEDDI | 1810 | Births | 1824-37 | 3790 |

## BRECON

| | | | | | |
|---|---|---|---|---|---|
| 1 | BRECON | | | | |
| | Watergate Chapel | 1807 | Births<br>Burials | 1806-37<br>1808, 1825 | } 3938 |
| 32 | TALACHDDU,<br>MAESYBERLLAN | 1699 | Births | 1803-37 | 3941 |

## CARDIGAN        [NONE]

## CARMARTHEN

| | | | | | |
|---|---|---|---|---|---|
| 5 | CARMARTHEN | | | | |
| | The Tabernacle,<br>formerly Dark Gate | 1660 | Births<br>Burials | 1785-1828<br>1790-1837 | } 3942 |
| | | | Births | 1827-37 | 4124 |

| | | Founded* | | | | RG 4/ |
|---|---|---|---|---|---|---|

7 CARMARTHEN
  Penuel Chapel,   1786   Births   1789-1837   4437
  Priory Street

- CWMNFELYN
  Llanwnio, Particular Baptist   Births   1779-1828
  Unauthenticated Register RG 8/103]

22 LLANELLY
  Tynewydd Felinfol   1709   Births   1775-1820   3821

42 LLANGYNOCK
  Ebenezer Chapel   1801   Births   1778-1837   3944

**CARNARVON**   [NONE]

**DENBIGH**

43 LLANFUROG
  Mwrog Street Chapel   1800   Births   1792-1830   3530
    Births   1824-37   4115

71 RUABON
  Pen-y-cae   1796   Births   1789-1837   3490

91 WREXHAM
  Old Meeting House,   1708   Births   1785-90
  Chester Street   Burials   1785-91   }   3868
    Births   1790-1837
    Burials   1791-94   }   3869

**FLINT**

31 RHUDDLAN   Births   1815-37   3949

## GLAMORGAN

| 1 | ABERDARE | | | | |
|---|---|---|---|---|---|
| | Carmel Chapel | 1806 | Births | 1806-37 | |
| | | | Deaths | 1814-36 | } 4117 |

| 38 | BRIDGEND | | | | |
|---|---|---|---|---|---|
| | Ruhamah Chapel, Newcastle | 1789 | Births | 1799-1837 | 3502 |

| 7 | CARDIFF | | | | |
|---|---|---|---|---|---|
| | Bethany Chapel, St Mary Street | 1806 | Births | 1804-16 | |
| | | | Deaths | 1807-16 | } 3879 |
| | | | Births | 1804-37 | |
| | | | Deaths | 1807-37 | } 3493 |

| 27 | MERTHYR TYDVIL | | | | |
|---|---|---|---|---|---|
| | Bethel Chapel, Georgetown | 1807 | Births | 1810-37 | 3499 |

| 36 | NEATH | | | | |
|---|---|---|---|---|---|
| | Bethany | 1770 | Births | 1773-1837 | 3950 |

| 45 | SWANSEA | | | | |
|---|---|---|---|---|---|
| | Mount Pleasant Meeting House | 1826 | Births | 1811-37 | 3503 |

| 44 | SWANSEA | | | | |
|---|---|---|---|---|---|
| | York Place Chapel | 1830 | Births | 1801-37 | 2667 |

## MERIONETH

| 10 | DOLGELLY | | | | |
|---|---|---|---|---|---|
| | Juda, West Street, Particular Baptist | 1798 | Births | 1798-1836 | |
| | | | Baptisms | 1800-35 | } 3898 |

|   | | Founded* | | | RG 4/ |
|---|---|---|---|---|---|
| - | LLANUWCHLLYN | | Baptisms | 1831-33 | 3898 |
| - | LLYNGWRIL | | Baptisms | 1832 | 3898 |

**MONTGOMERY**

| 14 | LANDRINIO | | | | |
|---|---|---|---|---|---|
| | Sarnwen Chapel | 1829 | Births | 1832-36 | 3905 |
| 10 | LLANIDLOES | | | | |
| | Particular Baptist | 1810 | Births | 1804-37 | 3958 |

**PEMBROKE**

| 19 | LLANGUM BURTON [= LLANGWM] | | | | |
|---|---|---|---|---|---|
| | Galilee Chapel | 1820 | Births | 1820-36 | 2491 |

| 20 | MILFORD | | | | |
|---|---|---|---|---|---|
| | Short Lane Chapel | 1828 | | | |
| | and Enon, SANDY | | Births | 1803-36 | 3476 |
| | HAVEN, ST ISHMAEL | 1814 | | | |

| - | MOLESTON: see NARBERTH, RG 4/3964 |
|---|---|

| 22 | NARBERTH | | | | |
|---|---|---|---|---|---|
| | Bethesda | 1817 | Births | 1807-37 | 3963 |
| 23 | NARBERTH | | | | |
| | Moleston Chapel | 1768 | Births | 1787-1837 | 3964 |
| 27 | PEMBROKE DOCK | | | | |
| | Bethany Chapel | 1818 | Births | 1814-37 | 3965 |

| - | SANDY HAVEN: see MILFORD, RG 4/3476 |
|---|---|

**RADNOR**                     [NONE]

# APPENDIX 2

## A LIST OF THE BAPTIST REGISTERS INCLUDING PARTICULAR, GENERAL AND UNITARIAN BAPTISTS OF WHICH COPIES ARE HELD IN THE LIBRARY OF THE SOCIETY OF GENEALOGISTS

Compiled by SUSAN GIBBONS, BA, ALA
Librarian of the Society of Genealogists

This listing follows the conventions of the Library and its published guides, in that county names are those in use before the 1974 re-organisation of local government. In London only places within the City of London are shown; places outside the boundaries of the City are listed under the ancient counties in which they were situated (ie: Essex, Kent, Middlesex and Surrey), for example Deptford appears under Kent and Southwark under Surrey.

**Abbreviations:** A = Adult Baptisms; B = Burials; C = Baptisms; D = Deaths; Ext = Extracts; (I) = Index; M = Marriages; R = Infant Naming (Registration or Dedication; Z = Births.

**Shelf Marks** are enclosed in square brackets [ ]. **[P]** indicates that the entry is to be found in a periodical. **Mf** and **mfc** are microfilms and microfiche respectively.

## BIBLIOGRAPHIES

A Baptist bibliography: being a register of the chief materials for Baptist history, whether in manuscript or in print, preserved in England, Wales and Ireland, vol. 1, 1526-1776 and vol. 2, 1777-1837 & Addenda from 1613 [NC/BAP/GEN]

## BIOGRAPHIES

A Baptist bibliography: being a register of the chief materials for Baptist history, whether in manuscript or in print, preserved in England, Wales and Ireland, vol. 1, 1526-1776, , vol. 2, 1777-1837 & Addenda from 1613 [NC/BAP/GEN]

Baptists who made history: a book about great Baptists written by Baptists [NC/BAP/GEN]

The Baptists' who's who: an authoritativ reference work & guide to the careers of ministers & lay officers of the Baptist churches [for 1933 (only)] [NC/BAP/DIR]

The signatories of the Orthodox Confession of 1679: 1$^{st}$ published in *Th Baptist Quarterly* vol. 17 1957 [NC/BAP/GEN]

## MINISTERS

Are listed in the Baptists Handbooks and Baptists Union Directories

Obituaries & marriages of dissenting ministers in the Gentleman's Magazine in the 18th century [NC/GEN, PER/GEN]

## DIRECTORIES

The Baptist hand-books for 1862-73, 1875-85,1887-90, 1892-1900, 1921, 1929, 1940, 1944-46 & 1949 [NC/BAP/DIR]

The Baptist union directories for 1977-89 [Winter Palace]

The Baptist Union directory for 1989-90 [NC/BAP/DIR]

The Baptists' who's who: an authoritative reference work & guide to the careers of ministers & lay officers of the Baptist churches [for 1933] [NC/BAP/DIR]

The General Baptist Church of Berkhamstead, Chesham & Tring, 1712-81: English Baptist records, no. 1 [NC/BAP/DIR]

## HISTORY

Baptists in Yorkshire; being the centenary memorial volume of the Yorkshire Baptist Association: Baptists in Yorkshire, Lancashire, Cheshire & Cumberland [NC/BAP/GEN]

Baptists of North West England, 1649-1913 [& North Wales] [NC/BAP/GEN]

Baptised believers: Lincolnshire Baptists in times of persecution, revolution & toleration 1600-1700 [LI/G 40]

Association life of the Particular Baptists of Northern England 1699-1732: English Baptist records, no. 3 [NC/BAP/LST]

## REGISTERS

Dr. Williams' library protestant dissenters registry: Z 1767-1837: Vital records index British Isles on CD-ROM: ZCM 1538-1888 [Apply to library staff CD-ROM cabinet]

## ENGLAND

## BEDFORDSHIRE

Registers
**BEDFORD** (Mill Street): Z 1792-1836 [Apply to staff (mfc)]
**BIGGLESWADE** (Old Meeting): Z 1762-1837, B 1786 [Apply to staff (mfc)]
**BLUNHAM** (Particular): Z 1709-1837, B 1793-1827 [Apply to staff (mfc)]
**BLUNHAM** (Old Meeting chapel): chapel book 1724-1891, including Z 1773-74, C 1738-1801, D 1739-1806, 1860-90, B 1852-90 [BE/R 46]

**CARDINGTON**: ZC 1806-37
[Apply to staff (mfc)]
**CRANFIELD**: Z 1799-1837,
B 1794-1837 [Apply to staff (mfc)]
**DUNSTABLE** Z 1769-1836,
B1794-1837 [Apply to staff (mfc)]
**HOUGHTON REGIS**: Z 1769-1836,
B1794-1837 [Apply to staff (mfc)]
**LEIGHTON BUZZARD** (Lake Street):
Z 1771-1835, B1785-1835
[Apply to staff (mfc)]
**LUTON**: Z 1777-1837, B 1786-1837
[Apply to staff (mfc)]
**RIDGMONT**: Z 1782-1838
[Apply to staff (mfc)]
**SHEFFORD HARDWICK**: Z 1828-35
[Apply to staff (mfc)]
**SOUTHILL**: Z 1791-1834, B 1802-20
[Apply to staff (mfc)]
**SOUTHILL (Independent, later
Baptist Church): church book
1693-1851 [includes notes of some
adult baptisms & deaths] [BE/R 46]**
**SOUTHILL**: C 1538-1666, M
1549-1670, B 1544-1681, CMB 1704-12
extracts: Genealogia Bedfordiensis,
supplement [BE/G 27]
**STAUGHTON, LITTLE**: Z 1771-1811,
B 1786-1806 [Apply to staff (mfc)]
**WESTONING**: Z 1810-36
[Apply to staff (mfc)]
**WOOTTON**: Z 1828-37
[Apply to staff (mfc)]
Monumental Inscriptions
**BEDFORD** (Mill Street): [BE/M 34]
**BIGGLESWADE**: burial ground
[BE/M 38]
**CRANFIELD** (Merchants Lane): burial
ground [BE/M 33]; (Independent)
[BE/M 38]
**DUNSTABLE** (West Street):
[BE/M 34]

**KEYSOE BROOK END**: burial
ground [BE/M 4]
**TODDINGTON**: chapel yard [BE/L 9]

**BERKSHIRE**
Registers
**FARINGDON** (Anabaptists):
1678-1766 [BK/R 59]
**WALLINGFORD** (Thames Street):
Z1794-1837, B1796-1837
[Apply to staff (mfc)]
**WOKINGHAM**: B 1842-1917
(ext) [BK/M 17]
Monumental Inscriptions
**BEECH HILL**: [Apply to staff
(Shelf 9]
**MORETON, SOUTH** (Strict):
[Apply to staff (mfc)]
**READING**: Burial Ground [BK/M 17]
**WALLINGFORD**: [Apply to staff
(mfc)]; (Thames St) [BK/M 18];
graveyard [BK/M 18]
**WANTAGE** (Garston Lane
cemetery):[BK/M 13]
**WINDSOR** (Victoria Street):
[BK/M 18]

**BUCKINGHAMSHIRE**
General
The general Baptist Church of
Buckinghamshire, Chesham & Tring,
1712-81 [NC/BAP/DIR]
Registers
**CHALFONT ST PETER** (Gold Hill):
Z 1779-1836 in Origins vol. 6 no. 2,
Summer 1982 [BU/PER]
**DRAYTON PARSLOW**: C 1806, M
1806,1825, B 1833, members list at 25
Dec 1830 [BU/R 109]
**MURSLEY**: members list at 25 Dec
1830 [BU/R 109]

**NEWTON LONGVILLE**: CMB (I) 1755-1838, members list at 25 Dec 1830 [BU/R 109]
**PRINCES RISBOROUGH**: Z 1796-1837 [BU/R 97]
**SPEEN** (nr Aylesbury): D 1813-37 [BU/R 97]
**SWANBOURNE**: CMB (I) 1784-1833, c 1813-21[BU/R 109], members list at 25 Dec 1830 at 25 Dec 1830 [BU/R 109]

Monumental Inscriptions
**AMERSHAM, OLD** (The Platt): outside Chapel [BU/M 12]
**ASTON CLINTON** (Green End St): chapel yard [BU/M 8]
**BUCKLAND COMMON**: [BU/R 26]
**CHENIES**: graveyard [BU/M 12, BU/M 8]
**CHESHAM** (Hinton): [BU/M 1], (Trinity) at rear of chapel [BU/M 11]
**CRENDON, LONG**: MIs (I) [BU/M 8]
**HADDENHAM**: [war memorials & war graves] in burial ground 1919, 1941-42 [BU/M 18]
**HYDE HEATH**: [war memorial memorials & war graves] in chapel 1914-18 [BU/M 18]
**IVINGHOE**: chapel yard [BU/M 9]
**KINGSHILL, LITTLE**: [war memorial memorials & war graves] chapel yard 1943 [BU/M 18]
**LEDBURN**: NO MIs [BU/M 12]
**LONG CRENDON** - see **CRENDON, Long.**
**MARLOW** (Glade Road): Building inscriptions (NO MIs) [BU/M 11]
**MISSENDEN, GREAT** (Trafford Road cemetery): [BU/M 2], [war memorial memorials & war graves] 1919 [BU/M 18]

**PRINCES RISBOROUGH**: MIs, list of members' names 1862-63 [BU/M 15]
**QUAINTON**: [BU/M 16]
**WADDESDON HILL** (Strict): burial ground [BU/M 12]
**WINCHMORE HILL** (St Andrew): NO MIs [BU/M 11]
**WYCOMBE, HIGH** (Oakridge Road): outside Chapel [BU/M 12]
**WYCOMBE, HIGH** (The Pastures, Mount Zion): Building inscription [BU/M 12]; (Easton Street, Union): outside chapel [BU/M 12]

**CAMBRIDGESHIRE**
General
**CAMBRIDGE** (St. Andrew's St): Church Book 1720-1832 [NC/BAP/DIR]
Registers
**BOTTISHAM LODE**: Z (I) 1809-36 [Apply to staff (mfc)]
**GAMLINGAY**: Z 1815-37 [Apply to staff (mfc)]
**WILLINGHAM** C 1754-1827, Z 1781-1820, D 1728-49; list of deacons 1662-1844 [CA/R 80]
**WISBECH**: Z1700-1837, C 1711-50, M 1715-49, B 1706-55 [CA/R 160]; M(I) 1715-21, 1726, 1731-49, 1784, 1792, 1818 & 1838 [CA/R 117, 138 & Boyd's marriage index]
Monumental Inscriptions
**BURWELL** [Apply to staff (mfc)]
**ELSWORTH** (Strict): [CA/M 8]
**FULBOURN** (Old Chapel): [CA/M 7]
**GAMLINGAY** (Old Meeting): [CA/M 8]
**GRANSDEN, GREAT**: [CA/M 8]
**HADDENHAM** (cemetery): MIs (I) [CA/ M 1]
**HARSTON** [CA/M 10]

**LODE**: graveyard [CA/M 4]
**MELBOURN**: [CA/M 21]
**SUTTON IN THE ISLE**: [CA/M 21]
**CHESHIRE**
General
**BRAMHALL & WARFORD,
GREAT**: A peep into Baptist history in
Cheshire [CH/R 31]
Registers
**DUCKINFIELD**: M 1677-1713
[CH/R 33], CMB 1677-1713 (ext):
Transactions of the Historic Society of
Lancashire & Cheshire, vol. 33
[LA/PER]
**WARFORD, GREAT**: C1750,
1757-61, 1785, 1792-1829, 1836-54 B
1802, 1808-60, 1880-1929 [CH/R 31]
Monumental Inscriptions
**BRAMHALL**: [Apply to staff (mfc)]
**BUDWORTH, GREAT**: (Appleton,
Hill Cliff Chapel): (ext) [CH/R 46]
**MOTTRAM COMMON**: Burial
ground [Mf 1104]
**WARFORD, GREAT**
[Apply to staff (mfc)]

**CORNWALL**
Registers
**HELSTON**: Z 1805-37 [CO/R 23]
**PADSTOW** (Coinage St): Z 1826
[CO/R 25]
**SCILLY ISLES**: ZC 1819-37
[CO/R 26]
**TRURO** (Kenwyn St): ZC 1760-1837
[CO/R 27]
Monumental Inscriptions
**CALSTOCK**: [CO/M 17]
**ST AUSTELL**: [CO/M 17]
**SALTASH**: [CO/M 12]

**DERBYSHIRE**
Registers
**DERBY**: Z extracts 1814-23, C 1823-37
[DB/R 60]
**STONEBROOM**: roll book 1877-80
[DB/R 63]
**WINGFIELD, SOUTH** (Birches Lane):
Roll Book 1878-1956, B 1938-94
[DB/R 63]
**WIRKSWORTH**: ZC 1824-37
[DB/R 48, Mf 2371]
Monumental Inscriptions
**CASTLE GRESLEY** (Mount Pleasant):
Foundation stone inscriptions 1882
[DB/M 19]
**DERBY** (Agard St): burial ground
[DB/M 2]
**DUFFIELD**: [Apply to staff (mfc)];
(General): [DB/M 3]
**ILKESTON** (South St): chapel yard
[DB/M 7]
**LANGLEY MILL**: burial ground
[includes Boer War memorial]
[DB/M 4, 12]
**LOSCOE**: [DB/M 23]
**MEASHAM**: chapel yard [LE/M 5]
**RIPLEY**: [Apply to staff (mfc)]
**SAWLEY**: [DB/M 23]

**DEVONSHIRE**
General
A book of remembrance: or a short
history of the Baptist churches in North
Devon [DE/G 3]
Registers
**APPLEDORE** (Northam): Z 1834-37
[DE/R 94]; (Ebenezer Chapel) Z1834-37
[Mf 2376]
**ASHWATER**: Z 1828-37 [Mf 2372]

**BAMPTON** (High St): Z 1807-37, B 1827 [Mf 2376 & DE/R 95]
**BARNSTAPLE** (Vicarage Lane): Z 1821-37 [DE/R 94, Mf 2376]
**BOVEY TRACEY** (Hen St): Z 1778-1837, B 1784-1837 [Mf 2376]; Z 1778-1837 B 1784-93, 1798-1826, 1831-37 [DE/R 95]
**BRAYFORD**: Z 1831-37 [DE/R 95]; (Particular): Z 1831-37 [Mf 2377]
**CROYDE** (Particular): C 1821-35 [DE/R 96]
**CULMSTOCK** (Prescott Chapel): Z1787-1836, B 1789-1836 [Mf 2378]; [DE/R 96]
**DEVONPORT** (Liberty St & Pembroke St): ZC 1779-1820 [Mf 2379 & DE/R 97]; (Morice Sq, Plymouth Dock): Z 1770-1837 [Mf 2370], [DE/R 96]
**DODBROOKE** (Refuge Chapel): Z 1819-36 [Mf 2361]
**EXETER** (South St): Z 1776-1837 [Mf 2361]
**GEORGEHAM** (Particular): Z 1821-35 [Mf 2378]
**HONITON** (Particular): C 1829-37 [Mf 2362]
**SAINTHILL** (Kentisbeare): Z 1806-36 [Mf 2366]
**KINGSBRIDGE**: Z 1785-1813, B 1785-1837 [Mf 2366]
**PLYMOUTH** (How St): Z 1786-1837, B 1787-1837 [Mf 2367]
**STONEHOUSE** (Ebenezer Chapel, Union St): Z 1833-36 [Mf 2365]
**THORVERTON**: M1852-85, B 1843-1909 [DE/L 69]
**TIVERTON** (Newport St): Z 1767-1837, B 1816-37 [Mf 2368]

Monumental Inscriptions
**AUTON GIFFORD** (Venn): burial grounds [DE/M 23]
**BRAYFORD**: [DE/M 17]
**HEMYOCK**: B 1860-1967 [DE/M 18]
**KINGSBRIDGE** (Church Lane & Phoenix Place): cemeteries [DE/M 23]

**DORSET**
Registers
**BROADWINSOR** (Venn Chapel): C 1843-57, D 1852-94, B 1851-61 [DO/R 101]; (Stony Napps, Ebenezer): Cc. 1864-97, D 1878-95, B 1862-91 [DO/R 101]
**CHARD**: a list of all the members of the Baptist church of Chard, Dorset, as listed 21 Dec 1783 [Mf 2835]
Monumental Inscriptions
**BUCKLAND NEWTON** (Henley Chapel): MIs [DO/M 17]

**DURHAM**
Registers
Pre 1837 non-anglican marriages. [Irregular marriages 1754-1837] [Apply to staff (mfc)]
**CHIRBURY**: C(I) 1827-34 [Apply to staff (mfc)]
**HAMSTERLY**: C 1729-65, CD 1771-1848 [NU/R 32]; B(I) 1813-37 [Apply to staff (mfc)]; C(I) 1750-1837 [Apply to staff (mfc)]
**MIDDLETON IN TEESDALE**: C(I) 1829-37 [Apply to staff (mfc)]
**MUGGLESWICK** (Rowley): B(I) 1813-37 [Apply to staff (mfc)]
**ROWLEY**: C(I) 1778-1836 [Apply to staff (mfc)]

**SHIELDS, SOUTH**: C(I) 1796-1836 [Apply to staff (mfc)]
**SUNDERLAND**: C(I) 1797-1837 [Apply to staff (mfc)]
Monumental Inscriptions
**HAMSTERLEY**: chapel yard [DU/M 17]
**HAMSTERLEY ROWLEY**: [Apply to staff (mfc)]
**ROWLEY** or **COLD ROWLEY** (Castleside): [DU/M 6]
**WOLSINGHAM**: [Apply to staff (mfc)]

**ESSEX**
Local
**THAXTED**: notes (includes abstracts of PCC wills 1546-1829, list of clergy 1314-1752, MIs in the church & churchyard & on the tombstones of the Congregational & Baptist chapels, extracts from directories for 1832 & 1838 & the 1841 census return) [ES/L 37]
Registers
**RAYLEIGH**: B 1874-1922, D 1874-1913, 1922-25 [ES/M 8]
**SAFFRON WALDEN** (General): Z 1827-37 [ES/R 19]
Monumental Inscriptions
**LANGHAM** [ES/M 4]
**RAMSDEN BELLHOUSE**: [Apply to staff - Shelf 9]
**RAYLEIGH**: [ES/M 8]
**SAFFRON WALDEN** (High St): chapel yard 1772-1866 [ES/M 2]; (London Road, Strict) chapel yard , lists of members [includes dates of death] 1820-50, 1855-66, 1872-91, 1900-05, B 1857-76 [ES/M 2]
**THAXTED**: [ES/L 37]
**TILLINGHAM**: burial ground [ES/M 1]

**GLOUCESTERSHIRE**
Registers
**BROADMEAD**: the records of a Church of Christ in Bristol, 1640-87: Bristol Record Society's Publications, vol. 27 [GL/PER]
**CHIPPING SODBURY**: B 1771-1988 [Apply to staff – Shelf 9]
Monumental Inscriptions
**ASHCHURCH** (Natton, 7th Day Baptist burial ground): [GL/M 44 & 46]
**BRISTOL** (Broadmead Meeting House): (extr) [GL/ M44]; (Downend): [GL/M 8], (Fishponds): [GL/M 4]; (Old King St): vaults [GL/M 21], (Redcross St): [one entry only] [GL/M 33]
**CHELTENHAM** (Knapp Road, St James' Square, Bethel graveyard): [GL/M 46]
**CHIPPING SODBURY** [GL/M 26]; [Apply to staff - Shelf 9]
**CODRINGTON**: Dedication stones [GL/M 43]; [Apply to staff - Shelf 9]
**FOUR OAKS nr DYMOCK**: [GL/M 44]
**HANHAM**: burial ground [GL/M 11]
**PAULTON**: graveyard [GL/M 28]
**SODBURY, OLD**: [Apply to staff - Shelf 9]
**STROUD** (London Road): [GL/M 17]
**TEWKESBURY** (Barton St): burial ground [GL/M 23]; (Old Baptists): graveyard [GL/M 31]
**WESTERLEIGH** (Grace Evangelical): [Apply to staff - Shelf 9]; (Tabernacle): [Apply to staff - Shelf 9]
**WOODCHESTER**: inside chapel [GL/M 23]
**WOTTON UNDER EDGE** (Old Town): inside chapel [GL/M 23]

# HAMPSHIRE
<u>Registers</u>
**ANMORE** (Hambledon): Z 1820-37
[HA/R 113]
**NEWPORT** (Protestant Dissenting
Meeting House (General): Z 1739-1837
[HA/R 114]
**PORTSMOUTH** (St Thomas' St): ZB
1785-1836 [HA/R 114]
<u>Monumental Inscriptions</u>
**BROUGHTON**: [HA/M 9]
**FLEET** (Hope Cemetery): chapel yard
[HA/M 10]
**SPEARYWELL**: [4 entries only]
[HA/M 6]
**SWAY**: chapel yard [HA/M 6]

# HEREFORDSHIRE
<u>Registers</u>
**FOWNHOPE**: Z 1827-35, with
admissions & removals 1837-61
[Apply to staff – Box 28/folder 2]
**GORSLEY**: Z 1831-37 [HR/R 13]
**HEREFORD**: C 1832-37 [HR/R 13]
**KINGTON**: ZC 1791-1837 [HR/R 13]
**LEOMINSTER**: C 1733-1836,
B 1702-1836 [HR/R 13]
**WESTON UNDER PENYARD**: Z
1787-1837, B 1791-1836 [HR/R 13]
<u>Monumental Inscriptions</u>
**GARWAY**: [HR/M 11 & 12]
**HEREFORD** (Zion Chapel): graveyard
[HR/M 10]
**KINGSLAND**: Disused chapel - NO
inscriptions [HR/M 12]
**ROSS ON WYE** (Strict):
(NO Inscriptions) [HR/M 14]
**STANSBATCH** (nr Staunton on Arrow):
[HR/M 10]
**WHITESTONE**: [HR/M12]

# HERTFORDSHIRE
<u>General</u>
The General Baptist Church of
Berkhamstead, Chesham & Tring, 1712-
81: English Baptist records, no. 1
[NC/BAP/DIR]
<u>Local</u>
**HITCHIN** (Tilehouse Street, Bunyan
Church): Chapel book [HT/L 18]
<u>Registers</u>
**BERKHAMSTED**: Z(I) 1799-1837,
B(I) 1801-83 [HT/R 52]
**HATFIELD** (Park Street, Union of
Independents & Baptists): ZC 1823-54,
B 1846-1920, MIs [HT/R 57]
<u>Monumental inscriptions</u>
**ASHWELL** (Zoar):
[Apply to staff – Shelf 9] [HT/M 2]
**BERKHAMSTED, GREAT**
(burial ground): [Mf 343, 344 & 347]
**BERKHAMSTED**: [HT/M 5]
**BOXMOOR**: [HT/M 5, 8 & Mf 344]
**BREACHWOOD GREEN**:
burial ground [Mf 350]
**CHIPPERFIELD**: burial ground
[Mf 345 & 347]
**FLAMSTED**: burial ground
[Mf 344 & 347]
**FLAUNDEN**: burial ground [HT/M 1]
**GADDESDEN, GREAT**: burial ground
[Mf 344 & 347]
**GADDESDEN ROW** (Ebenezer):
[HT/M 8]
**HATFIELD**: [Mf 339]
**HEMEL HEMPSTEAD** (Crown Yard):
burial ground [HT/M8]
**HITCHIN** (Tilehouse Street) [HT/M 24]
**MARKYATE STREET**: burial ground
[Mf 345 & 347]
**REDBOURN** (Particular): burial ground
Mf 346, 349 & HT/M 24]

**SARRATT** [HT/M 27]
**ST ALBANS**: burial ground [Mf 348]
**TRING**: burial ground [Mf 345 & 347]

**HUNTINGDONSHIRE**
Monumental Inscriptions
**HUNTINGDON** (Warboys Chapel):
chapel yard [HU/M 3]
**PERRY**: [Apply to staff (mfc)]
**SOMERSHAM**: [HU/M 2]
**ST. NEOTS**: [HU/M 6]
**STAUGHTON, GREAT**:
[Apply to staff (mfc)]
**WARBOYS** - see **HUNTINGDON**

**KENT**
Local
**SMARDEN** (Zion Chapel, General):
notes on elders & ministers [KE/M 10]
Registers
**BESSELS GREEN** (General): Z 1682-
1815, M 1840-53, B 1738/9-1861
[KE/R 227]
**BETHERSDEN**: Z 1799-1836
[Apply to staff (mfc)]
**BEXLEYHEATH**: B 1831-32
[KE/R 227]
**CANTERBURY** (Black Friars): C
1780-1815, B 1785-1836 (ext)
[KE/R 227 & Apply to staff - Shelf 9]
**CHATHAM** (General): Z 1700-1837
B1785-1837, Membership Register
1750 [KE/R 256]
**CRANBROOK** (General): Z1682-
1700, 1712-77, D 1809-37 [KE/R 273]
**DEPTFORD**: B 1824-34 & MIs
[Apply to staff (mfc)]
**EGERTON**: B 1863-1984
[Apply to staff (mfc)]
**EYNSFORD**: ext CMB 1813-37
[Apply to staff (mfc)]

**EYTHORNE**: Z 1723-1837
[Apply to staff (mfc)], D 1797-1858,
memorial roll 1850-1858
[Apply to staff (mfc)]
**HEADCORN** (Rumpton Chapel, Love
Lane to c. 1819) (General to c. 1819,
Unitarian since 1819): Z 1731-1837,
M 1765-1830, B 1780-1837, D
1819-37& pedigrees of the Love,
Boorman & Diprose families
[KE/R 273]
**LESSNESS HEATH**: C 1807-29,
B 1808-22 [KE/R 231]
**ROLVENDEN**: ZC 1796-1834
[KE/R 234]
**SMARDEN**: M 1840-1984,
B 1837-1984 [Apply to staff (mfc)]
**TENTERDEN**: B 1870-1983
[Apply to staff (mfc)]
Monumental Inscriptions
**BRABOURNE**: burial ground [KE/M 7]
**BROADSTAIRS, ST PETERS,**
(Salem): MIs 1800-1937 [KE/M 7]
**CROCKENHILL** (Darns Hill Old
Burial Ground) [KE/M 64],
(Union Burial Ground & Darns Hill Old
Burying Ground) [Apply to staff (mfc)],
(Union): [KE/M 61]
**FOLKESTONE** (Bradstone Road):
burial ground [KE/PER]
**FOOTS CRAY**: [Apply to staff (mfc)
KE/MI/67293/1]; [KE/M 1]
**HEADCORN**: [KE/M 68]
**SANDHURST**: chapel yard
[KE/M 4 & 10]
**SMARDEN** (Tilden, Particular)
[KE/M 10]

# LANCASHIRE
Registers
**ACCRINGTON** (Machpelah): B 1806-17, 1834-34 (ext) & MIs [Apply to staff (mfc)]
**BLACKBURN** (Islington, Particular): B 1764-71, 1797-1837 [Apply to staff (mfc)]
**HAGGATE**: Z 1762-1841, b 1786-94, 1805, 1811-57 [Apply to staff (mfc)]
**INSKIP**: MIs; B(I) 1817-1996 [Apply to staff (mfc)]
**PRESTON, LONG**: M(I) 1883-86, 1891-98, 1904-14, 1922-30, 1939-57, B 1836, 1849-53, 1863-1965, 1971-85 [Apply to staff (mfc)]
Monumental Inscriptions
**ACCRINGTON** (Machpelah): burial ground [Mf 2917]
**BILLINGTON** (Ebenezer): [Apply to staff (mfc)]
**BRIERCLIFFE** (Haggate & Hill Lane Chapel, Nelson Road) [Apply to staff (mfc)]
**BURNLEY** (Haggate, including Hill Lane, Briercliffe): [LA/M 9]
**HAWKSHEAD HILL**: burial ground [LA/M 15]
**HURSTWOOD**: [Apply to staff (mfc)]
**OGDEN**: old churchyard [LA/M 2]
**OSWALDTWISTLE** (New Lane): [Apply to staff (mfc)]
**ROCHDALE** (Hope Street): gravestones of Town Meadows Chapel [Apply to staff (mfc)]
**SABDEN**: [Apply to staff (mfc)]

# LEICESTERSHIRE
Registers
**KNIPTON**: ZCMB 1609-1726 (ext) [LE/R 17]

**LEICESTER** (Archdeacon Lane): Z1811-14, C 1820-36, D(I) 1810-49, B(I) 1838-53; membership list 1809 [LE/R 14]; (Charles Street): B(I) 1831-81 [Apply to staff (mfc)]; (Upper Charles Street): DB 1831-37; list of ministers [LE/R 41]; (Dover Street): Z 1813-37 [LE/R 41]; (Friar Lane): Z 1785-1837, B 1787, 1789 [LE/R 41]; (Harvey Lane): Z 1791-1810, B 1805-37 [LE/R 41]; B(I) 1800-81 [Apply to staff (mfc)]
Monumental Inscriptions
**BARTON IN THE BEANS**: [LE/M 3]
**BILLESDON**: chapel yard [LE/M 7]
**DISEWORTH**: [Apply to staff (mfc)]
**HUGGLESCOTE**: burial ground; membership roll 1798-1841 [LE/M 3
**MEASHAM**: chapel yard [LE/M 5]
**MOUNTSORREL**: Old burial ground [LE/R 6 & LE/M 3]
**QUORN** (General): [LE/M 3, 5 & 14]
**ROTHLEY**: chapel yard [LE/M 3]
**SWITHLAND**: [LE/M 3]
**THURLASTON**: [Apply to staff (mfc)]
**WHATTON, LONG**: [LE/M 15]
**WOODHOUSE** (Evangelical): [LE/M 3]
**WOODHOUSE EAVES**: [LE/M 3]
**WYMESWOLD** (Old chapel): [LE/M 5]

# LINCOLNSHIRE
General
Baptised believers: Lincolnshire Baptists in times of persecution, revolution & toleration 1600-1700 [LI/G 40]
Registers
**KILLINGHOLME**: M(I) 1657-1853 [Apply to staff (mfc)]

Monumental Inscriptions
**BOSTON**: [LI/M 50]
**BURGH**: burial ground [LI/M 17]
**CARLTON le MOORLAND** (Old Burial Ground): [LI/M 50]
**CONINGSBY**: [LI/M 50]
**CROWLE**: chapel yard [LI/M 22 & 61]
**EPWORTH**: [LI/M 34]
**FLEET**: [LI/M 18]
**GRIMSBY** (Victoria St, Tabernacle): War Memorial 1914-18 [LI/M 18]
**KILLINGHOLME, SOUTH**: burial ground [LI/M 53]
**MONKSTHORPE**: graveyard [LI/M 30]
**SUTTON, LONG**: [LI/M 27]
**SUTTON ST. JAMES**: chapel yard [LI/M 28]

**LONDON/MIDDLESEX**
Local
**LONDON** (Mill Yard Seventh Day Baptist): Church records 1673-1964 [Mf 627]
**LONDON** (Pinner's Hall Seventh Day Baptist): Chapel records 1686-1863 [Mf 626]
**HARROW**: The Harrow Baptist Church 1806-1956 [Includes lists of ministers 1812-1954] [MX/L 226]
Registers
**BISHOPSGATE** (Universal): Z 1789-1811 [MX/R 263]
**HAMMERSMITH** (Ebenezer): Z 1760-1835, C 1773-1835, B 1786-87 [Apply to staff (mfc)]; (Trinity, West End): Z 1780-1837, C 1783-1837, B 1784-1837 [Apply to staff (mfc)]

**HARROW ON THE HILL**: Z 1826-36, C 1831-36 [Apply to staff (mfc)]
Monumental Inscriptions
**POTTERS BAR**: MIs(I) [MX/M 96-98]

**NORFOLK**
**NORWICH** (St Mary): The account of the "baptized" church in the city of Norwich 1726-45: Norfolk Record Society, vol. 22 [NF/PER]
Registers
**BACTON**: B 1826-36 [Apply to staff (mfc)]
**DISS** (Particular): Z 1806-36 [NF/R 80]
**ELLINGHAM, GREAT**: B 1817-37 [Apply to staff (mfc)]
**FOULSHAM**: B1823-25 [Apply to staff (mfc)]
**FRAMINGHAM PIGOT** (Particular): Z 1808-36 [NF/R 80]
**INGHAM**: B 1785-1821 [Apply to staff (mfc)]
**KINGS LYNN** (Stepney, Particular): B 1843-57 [Apply to staff (mfc)]
**NEATISHEAD** (Particular): CB 1801-37 [Apply to staff (mfc)]
**SAXLINGHAM THORPE** (Particular): Z 1793-1837 [NF/R 80]
**SHELFANGER** (Particular): Z 1795-1837 [NF/R 80]

**NORTHAMPTONSHIRE**
Registers
**KETTERING**: C 1785-1836 (ext), B 1785-1837 [NH/R 39]
**RINGSTEAD**: Z 1792-1836 [NH/R 25]
**THRAPSTON**: Z1783-1836, B 1794-1837 [NH/R 25]
**WELLINGBOROUGH**: ZC 1795-1837, DB 1792-1836 [NH/R 25]

Monumental Inscriptions
RAUNDS: [NH/M 1]

## NORTHUMBERLAND
Registers
BERWICK (Walkergate, Calvinistic):
C(I) 1805-37
[Apply to library staff (mfc)]
HEXHAM: C 1651-80[NU/R 32]
NEWCASTLE (Berwick Street): C(I)
1829-36 [Apply to staff (mfc)]; (Tuthill
Stairs): C(I) 1781-1837 [Apply to staff
(mfc)]; (Westgate St): C(I) 1806-37
[Apply to staff (mfc)]
SHIELDS, NORTH: C(I) 1790-1837
[Apply to staff (mfc)]
SUNDERLAND: C(I) 1797-1837
[Apply to staff (mfc)]
Monumental Inscriptions
BROOMHAUGH: burial ground
[NU/M 5]

## NOTTINGHAMSHIRE
Local
BASFORD, NEW (Pepper St): register
[of congregation] 1877-93] [NT/PER]
Registers
NOTTINGHAM (Bearward Lane,
burial ground) B 1787-1837 [NT/L 9];
(Friar Lane & George St): Z 1742-1836
[NT/L 9]
Monumental Inscriptions
COLLINGHAM: [NT/M 7 & 9]
KIRKBY WOODHOUSE (General):
[NT/M 8]
LANGLEY MILL (General): [NT/M 8]
LEAKE, EAST: chapel yard [NT/M 6]
NEWTHORPE: [NT/M 1 & 8]
NOTTINGHAM (Derby Road): war
memorial [NT/M 9], (Mount St): burial
ground [NT/L 9 & M 3]

RETFORD, EAST: [NT/M 10]
SOUTHWELL: [NT/M 12]

## OXFORDSHIRE
Registers
BURFORD (Witney Street): Z 1809-36,
B 1815-36 [OX/R 286]
CHIPPING NORTON: Z 1767-1831
[OX/R 286 & The Oxfordshire Family
Historian, vol. 3 no. 6, Autumn 1984
[OX/PER]
COTE (Bampton): Z 1647-1836, M
1775, 1839, DB 1657-1839; B 1840-88,
MIs in chapel; founder members 1656;
church members 1772-1881; list of
ministers 1703-1885 [OX/R 286]
HOOK NORTON: Z 1772-1839,
C1820-21, 1834-39, 1845, M 1844-49,
1872-77, B 1841-56, Lists of members
1609, 1706, 1728, 1743, 1755, 1811,
1823, 1839 & 1842 [OX/R 286]
SYDENHAM: C(I) 1821-37
[Apply to staff (mfc)]
SYDENHAM: Z 1821-37 [OX/R 287]
THAME: Z 1826-37, D 1828-36
[OX/R 287]
WITNEY: C 1799-1819
[Apply to staff (mfc)]
Z 1799-1835, C 1804-36, DB 1828,
1831 [OX/R 286]
Monumental inscriptions
CHADLINGTON: graveyard
[OX/M 8]
CHARLTON UPON OTMOOR:
graveyard [OX/M 8]
HEADINGTON: graveyard [OX/M 8]

## SHROPSHIRE
Registers
BRIDGNORTH (Castle St):
CB 1779-1836 [SH/R 1]

**BROSELEY** (Birchmeadow, Particular): Z 1835-37 [SH/R 104]; Z 1794-1835 [SH/R 1]
**CHIRBURY**: C(I) 1827-34 [Apply to staff (mfc)], (Particular): Z 1829-35 [SH/R 104]
**PONTESBURY**: CB 1828-36 [SH/R 104]
**SHIFNAL** (Aston St, Particular): Z 1811-36 [SH/R 104]
**SHREWSBURY** (Claremont Street): C 1766-1808 [SH/R 1], Z 1808-25 [SH/R 110]; Z 1813-36 [SH/R 104]
Monumental Inscriptions
**BROSELEY**: [SH/M 5]
**CHORLEY**: [SH/M 1]
**COXALL**: [SH/M 5]
**IGHTFIELD** (Mossfield): burial ground [SH/M 16]
**MAESBROOK**: [SH/M 12]
**MARKET DRAYTON**: [SH/M 2]
**PONTESBURY**: chapel yard [SH/M 16]
**WORTHEN** (Brockton): [SH/M 20]

**SOMERSET**
Local
**CHARD**: list of all the members 21 Dec 1783 [Mf 2835 & Somerset tracts box]
**WELLINGTON**: The materials for the history of the town of Wellington, co. Somerset (includes MIs in the parish church & Baptist chapel, register extracts parish church CMB 1683-1812 & Baptist chapel CD 1740-1807; & a list of clergy 1215-1889) [SO/L 26]
Registers
**FROME** (Badcox Lane): C 1834-1961; communicants list 1896 [Mf 1384] dates?

**WELLINGTON**: (ext) CD 1740-1807 & MIs [SO/L 26]
Monumental Inscriptions
**CHEW MAGNA**: [GL/M 10]
**ODCOMBE** (Five Ashes burial ground): [SO/M 17 & 41]
**PAULTON**: graveyard [GL/M 17]
**WINCANTON**: [SO/G 1 & SO/M 11]

**STAFFORDSHIRE**
Registers
**COSELEY** (Coppice, Particular): Z 1796-1837 [ST/R 120]; (Darkhouse): Z 1814-36 [ST/R 120]; (Providence): Z 1809-37, C 1810-34 [ST/R 120]
**WOLVERHAMPTON** (Walsall St): Z 1832-36 [ST/R 120]
Monumental Inscriptions
**BRIERLEY HILL** (South St): [ST/M 18]
**BURTON ON TRENT**: burial ground [ST/M 5]

**SUFFOLK**
Local
**LOWESTOFT**: London Road baptist church & Gunton baptist hall, yearbook, 1956 [Suffolk tracts box]
Registers
**BARDWELL** (Particular): Z 1817, 1820-37 [SF/R 257]
**CLARE**: B 1822-37 [SF/R 263]
**OTLEY: CMB(I)** in Suffolk Roots vol. 8 no. 2 [SF/PER]
Monumental Inscriptions
**CLARE**: chapel yard [SF/M 9]
**SOMERSHAM**: chapel [SF/M 13]
**WALTON** (Maidstone Road): [SF/M 19]

# SURREY
Registers
**BETCHWORTH** (Brockham): Z 1781-1837, C 1781-1827
[Apply to staff – Shelf 9]
**CHOBHAM**: Z 1810-36, DB 1824
[SR/R 21 & Apply to staff – Shelf 9]
**CLAPHAM** (Particular): Z 1781-1836
[Apply to staff – Shelf 9]; Z(I) 1781-1836 [SR/R 21]
**KINGSTON**(Particular): Z 1781-1837, D 1799-1836, B 1799-1836
[Apply to staff – Shelf 9]; Z 1781-1837, DB 1799-1836 [SR/R 21]
**SOUTHWARK** (Christchurch): Z(I) 1772-1826 [Mf 1427]
**WANDSWORTH** (Bridge Field): Z 1816-37, B 1825-36 [Apply to staff – Shelf 9]
Monumental Inscriptions
**CHARLWOOD** (Providence): chapel yard [SR/M 2]
**EPSOM** (Bugby, Strict): [SR/M 17]
**HORLEY** (Lee St): [SR/M 5]
**LINGFIELD** (Salem): chapel yard [SR/M 40]
**OUTWOOD**: [SR/M 3]

# SUSSEX
Registers: General
Sussex believers: Baptist marriage in the 17th & 18th centuries [SX/G 36]
Registers
**BILLINGSHURST** (General): D 1755-1980 & MIs [SX/R 175]
**BODLE STREET GREEN** (Hellingly, Ebenezer, Strict): C 1863-1901, B 1870-89; MIs [SX/PER]
**BRIGHTON** (Bond St, Salem Particular): ZC 1775-1835, Z 1834-37 [Apply to staff (mfc)]; Z 1775-1837, B 1783-1834 [SX/R 23 & Apply to staff (mfc)]

**DITCHLING** (General): C 1812-33, B 1821-36, 1874-1901 [SX/R 214]
**HAILSHAM:** ZC 1795-1837 [SX/R 23 & Apply to staff (mfc)]
**HELLINGLY** (Zoar): Z 1801-37 [SX/PER];
**HORSHAM**: B 1720-38, 1749-69 [SX/R 23]
**LEWES** (Particular): Z 1775-1836 [SX/R 23], 1779-1836 [Apply to staff (mfc)]
**ROTHERFIELD**: Z 1748-1836 [SX/R 23 & Apply to staff (mfc)]
**RYE**: Z 1789-1836, B 1768-1836 [SX/R 23 & Apply to staff (mfc)]
**UCKFIELD** (Rockhall Chapel): Z 1783-1836 1836 [SX/R 23 & Apply to staff (mfc)]
**WADHURST** (Shover's Green ): Z 1812-37, B 1832-36 [SX/R 23 & Apply to staff (mfc)]
**WISBOROUGH GREEN**: C 1821-35 [SX/R 214]
**WIVELSFIELD** (General): C 1789-1836 [SX/R 214 & Apply to staff (mfc)]; (Bethel Particular): C 1790-93, 1811, 1815, 1837, B 1790-93 [SX/R 214]; Z1771-1836 [Apply to staff (mfc)]; Z 1784-89, 1771-1802, 1806-36 [SX/R 22]
Monumental Inscriptions
**HADLOW DOWN** (Provident, Independent): [SX/M 29]
**HAILSHAM** (Upper Dicker, Zoar): chapel yard [SX/M 8]
**HANDCROSS** (Zoar Strict): [SX/M 2]
**HORSHAM** (General): burial ground [SX/M 9]
**TICEHURST**: [SX/M 7]
**WIVELSFIELD** (Bethel): chapel yard [SX/M 23]

## WARWICKSHIRE
Registers
**DRAYCOTT** (Bourton on Dunsmore):
C 1817-33 [WA/R 58]
**FOLESHILL** (Longford chapel general
Baptist new connexion): Z 1769-1837,
C1785-1814, 1823-29, 1835-37,
B 1801-37 [WA/R 4]
**KENILWORTH** (Abbey Hill):
C 1831-36 [WA/R 58]
Monumental Inscriptions
**ALCESTER**: [WA/M 40]
**BIRMINGHAM** (Zion): [WA/M 36]
**DUNCHURCH**: graveyard [WA/M 6]
**HENLEY IN ARDEN**: [WA/M 41]
**POLESWORTH**: chapel yard
[WA/M 7]
**STRATFORD UPON AVON**
(Payton St): chapel yard [WA/M 10]
**STUDLEY**: [WA/M 39]
**UMBERSLADE**: [WA/M 2]
**WOLSTON** (Dyer's Lane): [WA/M 5]

## WESTMORLAND
Registers
**KENDAL** (Unitarian): Z 1801-39
[WE/L 4]

## WILTSHIRE
Registers
**ALLINGTON** (Particular): Z 1826-37
[Mf 1828]
**BOWER CHALK**: A1842-1917,
D 1879-1937 [Mf 1827]
**BRADENSTOKE**: B 1872-1917
[Mf 1828]
**BRADLEY, NORTH**: Z 1787-1837,
B 1779-1837 [Mf 1828]
**BRADLEY, NORTH**: Z(I) 1776-1837,
B(I) 1837 [Apply to staff (mfc)]
**CHIPPENHAM**: Z 1789, 1801, 1808-
37 [Mf 1828]; Z(I) 1789-1837
[Apply to staff (mfc)]
**CHRISTIAN MALFORD**: D 1839-43,
1847-63 [Mf 1828]
**CRICKLADE**: D 1847-63 [Mf 1828]
**DEVIZES** (New): Membership book
1805-1947 (includes CMD) [WL/R
114]; (Particular): Z 1772-1837, B 1780-
1836 [Mf 1828]; Z(I) 1772-1837, D(I)
1804-18, 1835-36, B(I) 1780-1834
[Apply to staff (mfc)]
**DOWNTON** (Particular): Z 1767-1837,
B 1794-1836 [Mf 1828]; (South Lane):
Z(I) 1767-1837, B(I) 1794-1836
[Apply to staff ]
**KNOYLE**: CDB 1824-1952,
M 1839-1939 [Mf 1827]
**KNOYLE, EAST** (Particular): Z 1821-
37 [Mf 1828]; Z(I) 1821-37
[Apply to staff (mfc)]
**LUDGERSHALL**: Z 1817-37, D 1826-
35 [Mf 1828]; ZC(I) 1817-37,
B(I) 1826-34 [Apply to staff (mfc]
**MALMESBURY**: Z 1749-1837
[Mf 1828]
**MALMESBURY, EAST**: D 1847-63
[Mf 1828]
**MELKSHAM**: Z 1774-1837, B 1784-
1836 [Mf 1828]; ZB(I) 1774-1837
[Apply to staff (mfc)]
**NETHERAVON** (Particular): Z 1814-
37 [Mf 1828]
**NETTLETON**: Z 1827-36, D 1826,
1832 [Mf 1828]; Z(I) 1827-36, D(I)
1826-32 [Apply to staff (mfc)]
**PEWSEY**: D 1847-63 [Mf 1828]
**SALISBURY**: Z 1785-91, B 1786-1830
[Mf 1828], (Brown Street): ZC(I) 1763-
1837, B(I) 1786-1830
[Apply to staff  (mfc)]

**SEMLEY**: CDB 1824-1952, M 1839-1939 [Mf 1827]; Z(I) 1821-37 [Apply to staff (mfc)]
**TROWBRIDGE**: Z 1816-37, B 1822-37 [Mf 1828]; (Back Street): B(I) 1822-37 [Apply to staff (mfc)]; (Emmanuel): Z 1783-1808, B 1783-1808, A1760-1900, DB 1807-1900 [Mf 1827]
**WARMINSTER**: B 1812-36 [Mf 1828]; (North Row, Ebenezer): B(I) 1812-36 [Apply to staff (mfc)]
**WOOTTON BASSETT**: D 1839-43, 1847-63 [Mf 1828]
Monumental Inscriptions
**STRATTON GREEN**: [WL/M 5]
**SWINDON** (South St): graveyard [WL/M 5]

**WORCESTERSHIRE**
Registers
**BROMSGROVE** (Catshill): C 1830-37 [Apply to staff – Shelf 9]
**CRADLEY**: Z 1794-1837, C 1804-33, B 1805-37; **list of members**, seat rent book 1798, 1820-21 [WO/R 15]
**DUDLEY**: ZC 1816, 1824-37, D1814-37 [WO/R 19]
**NETHERTON** (Messiah): C 1654-1798 [WO/R 71]
**SHIPSTON ON STOUR**: Z 1783-1836 [WO/R 70]
Monumental Inscriptions
**BEWDLEY**: [WO/M 23]
**COOKHILL**: [WO/M 26]
**EVESHAM** (Cow St): [WO/M 4]

**YORKSHIRE**
Registers
**BARNOLDSWICK** (Bridge Chapel): Z 1785-1837, B 1785-1817 [YK/R 180]

**EARBY**: Z 1802-37 [YK/R 180]
**IDLE**: B(I) 1810-37 [YK/R 284]
**LOCKWOOD**: B 1832-1912, funerals 1832-65 [Apply to staff (mfc)]
**PRESTON, LONG**: M(I) 1884-1957, B 1836, 1849-53, 1863-1965, 1971-85 Apply to staff (mfc)]; B 1836, 1849-53, 1863-1965, 1971-85 [Apply to staff (mfc)]
Monumental Inscriptions
**HALIFAX** (Pellon Lane): graveyard [YK/M 33]
**HEBDEN BRIDGE** (Birchcliffe): burial ground (incomplete) [YK/M 33]
**HORSFORTH** (Cragg Hill (formerly Zion) Chapel): [YK/M 87]
**LOCKWOOD** (Reboboth): chapel yard [YK/M 3]
**MILNSBRIDGE**: graveyard [YK/M 85]
**MIRFIELD** (Zion): [YK/M 48]
**PRESTON, LONG**: [Apply to staff (mfc)]
**RAWDON CRAGG**: [YK/M 86]
**SALENDINE NOOK**: MIs (I) in graveyard sections A-E & M [YK/M 85]

**SCOTLAND**

**INVERNESS**
Registers
**KINGUSSIE & INSH**: Z 1817-54 (ext) [Mf 2631]

**WALES**

**ANGELSEY**
Registers
**LLANRHUDDLAD** (Rhydwyb): Z 1789-1836 [Apply to staff – Shelf 9]

## BRECKNOCKSHIRE
Registers
**TALACHDDU** (Maesyberllan,
Particular): Z 1803-37 [WS/R 68]
**YSTRAD RHONDDA** (Nebo
Particular): Z(I) 1795-1849, MIs
[Apply to staff (mfc)]
Monumental Inscriptions
**BUILTH WELLS** (West Street): chapel
porch [WS/M 30], (Victoria Road):
[Apply to staff – Box 84/folder 1]
**CRICKHOWELL** (Bethabara):
[HR/M 8]
**DEFYNNOG** (Sennybridge Sion
Chapel): graveyard [WS/M 25]
**GLASBURY** [Y Clas ar wy] (Pen yr
Heol): MIs (I) [WS/M 42]; MIs
[WS/M 13]
**LLANEGLWYS** (Ramah): [WD/M 30]
**LLANGAMMARCH** (Treflys, Salem):
[Apply to staff (mfc)]
**LLANGAMMARCH WELLS** (Treflys
Salem): graveyard [WS/M 30
**LLANGATTOCK** (Llwmws): chapel
yard [WS/M 30 & Apply to staff (mfc]
**LLANIGON** (Capel y Ffin, Glynfach):
[Apply to staff (mfc)]
**LLANWRTYD** (Zion): [includes War
memorial & obelisk]
[Apply to staff (mfc)]
**LLYWEL** (Horeb):
[Apply to staff (mfc)]
**PENDERYN** (Bethel):
[Apply to staff (mfc)]
**PENDERYN** (Siloam):
[Apply to staff (mfc)]; chapel yard
[WS/M 25]
**SENNYBRIDGE** (Defynnog, Sion):
graveyard [WS/M 25]
**TALACHDDU** (Maes y Berllan):
[Apply to staff (mfc)]; (Maesyberllan,
Particular): burial ground) [WS/M 29]

**TALGARTH** (Tabernacle Chapel)
[WS/M 25 & 42]
**TALYBONT ON USK** (Bethania):
chapel yard [WS/M 25]
**TRAIAN MAWR** (Llywel, Horeb):
chapel yard [WS/M25]

## CARDIGANSHIRE
Registers
**ABERYSTWYTH**: C(I) 1804-37
[Apply to staff (mfc)]
Monumental Inscriptions
**ABERAERON** (Siloam) no inscriptions
[WS/M 49]
**BRYNHAFOD GORS-GOCH**
(Llanwenog): [WS/M 48]
**CWMSUMLOG** (Llanbadarn Fawr,
Tabernacle): [WS/M 47]
**GOGINAN** (Llanbadarn Fawr, Jezreel):
[WS/M 47]
**PENRHYN-COCH** (Llanbadarn Fawr,
Horeb): [WS/M 47]

## CARMARTHENSHIRE
Monumental Inscriptions
**RHYDWILYM**: [WS/M 36]
**YSTRADFFIN** (Rhadirmwyn,
Landovery, Seion): burial ground
[WS/M 24]

## DENBIGHSHIRE
Registers
**CEFN BYCHAN** (Welsh): Z 1798-
1848, 1866; MIs, list of clergy 1803-65
[WS/R 175]
**CEFN MAWR** (Seion Welsh): Z 1790,
1800-36; MIs in the garden of rest
[WS/R 181]
**LLANFWROG** (Mwrog Street): Z
1792-1837; 1851 religious census
[WS/R 77]

**LLANNEFYDD** (Pentre): Z 1805-37; 1851 religious census [WS/R 78]
**LLANSANNAN** (Bethania): Z 1814-30; 1851 religious census [WS/R 78]

## GLAMORGAN
Local
**PETERSON-SUPER-ELY** (Croes-y-Parc): membership lists 1811-60 [Apply to staff (mfc)]
Registers
**ABERDARE** (Monk Street, Carmel Particular): Z 1806-37, D 1809-36 [Apply to staff (mfc)]
**CARDIFF** (St Mary Street, Bethany): Z 1804-37, D 1807-37 [WS/R 8]
Monumental Inscriptions
**BETTWS** (Sardis) [Apply to staff (mfc)]
 **BRIDGEND** (Ruhamah, Welsh): [Apply to staff (mfc)]
**BRIDGEND** (Penyfai, Smyrna): [Apply to staff (mfc)]
**CADOXTON JUXTA BARRY** (Philadelphia): [Apply to staff (mfc)]
**CAERPHILLY** (Tonyfelin): [WS/M 34]
**CARDIFF** (St Mary Street, Bethany): members **1805-64**; MIs [WS/R 66]; (The Hayes, Tabernacle Welsh): [Apply to staff (mfc)]
**CEFN CRIBBWR** (Nebo Welsh): [Apply to staff (mfc)]
**CHURCH VILLAGE** (Salem Welsh): [Apply to staff (mfc) & WS/M 36]
**HENGOED** (Welsh): [Apply to staff (mfc)]
**KENFIG HILL** (Pisgah): [Apply to staff (mfc), WS/M 20 & WS/M 11]

**KILLAY** (Siloam): [Apply to staff (mfc)]
**KNELSTON** (Providence): [Apply to staff (mfc)]
**LALESTON** (Bethel): chapel yard [WS/M20 & Apply to staff (mfc)]
**LISVANE**: [Apply to staff (mfc)]
**LLANDYFODWG** (Blackmill, Paran): [Apply to staff (mfc)]
**LLANTWIT FARDRE** (Salem): [Apply to staff (mfc)]
**LLANTWIT MAJOR** (Commercial Street, Bethel): [WS/M 34 & 36]
**NANTYFFYLON** (Salem): [Apply to staff (mfc) & WS/M 23]
**PENTYRCH** (Penuel) [Apply to staff (mfc)]
**PENYGRAIG** (Capel Soar, Ffrwdamos): [Apply to staff (mfc)]
**PETERSON SUPER ELY** (Croes y Parc): chapel yard [Apply to staff (mfc)]
**RHYDYFELIN** (Bethelem): [Apply to staff (mfc) & WS/M 36]
**TAFFS WELL** (Ainon): [Apply to staff (mfc)]
**TONGWYNLAIS** (Ainon): chapel yard [WS/M 23]
**TONYREFAIL**: [Apply to staff (mfc)]
**TREHAFOD** (Siloam): [Apply to staff (mfc)]
**TREHERBERT** (Libanus): [Apply to staff (mfc) & WS/M 36]
**WENVOE** (Twyn yr Odyn ): [Apply to staff (mfc)], (Zoar): [Apply to staff (mfc)]
**WHITCHURCH** (Ararat): [Apply to staff (mfc) & WS/M 36]
**WICK**: [Apply to staff (mfc)]

## MONMOUTHSHIRE
Monumental inscriptions
**ABERBARGOED** (Caersalem):
[Apply to staff (mfc)]
**BEDWAS** (Hephzebah): chapel yard
[WS/M 30 & Apply to staff (mfc)]
**BETTWS CEDEWAIN** (New Wells):
[WS/M 41]
**BLACKWOOD** (Argoed): chapel yard
[WS/M 26]
**BLACKWOOD** (Libanus): chapel yard
[WS/M 12]
**CAERLEON** ): chapel yard [WS/M 12]
**CAERPHILLY** (Tonyfelin):
[Apply to staff (mfc)]
**CAERWENT**: [WS/M 18]
**CASTELL Y BWCH** (Zoar): chapel
yard [WS/M 12]
**CASTLETON: [WS/M 12]**
**CWMCARN** (Nazareth Chapel): chapel
yard [WS/M12]
**EARLESWOOD** (Gaerllwyd):
WS/M 18]
**GLASCOED** (Mount Zion): grave yard
[WS/M 21]
**GOYTRE** (Saron): chapel yard
[WS/M 21]
**LLANGIBBY** (Bethel): grave yard
[WS/M 17]
**LLANGWM**: chapel yard [WS/M 18]
**LLANVACHES** (Bethany): chapel yard
[WS/M 13]
**LLANVETHERINE**: chapel yard
[WS/M 22]
**MICHAELSTONE Y FEDW** (Tirzah):
chapel yard [WS/M 14]
**MYNDDISLWYN** (Twyn Gwyn):
chapel yard [WS/M 28]
**NASH**: [WS/M 17], chapel yard
[WS/M 10]

**NEWPORT** (Charles Street): chapel
yard [WS/M 14], (Commercial Street):
chapel yard [WS/M 17]
**PANDY** (Zoar): chapel yard [WS/M 22]
**PENALT**: chapel yard [WS/M 33]
**PENYGARN**: [WS/M 30]; (Pontypool):
chapel yard [WS/M 19]
**PENYGRAIG**: [Apply to staff (mfc)]
**PONTHIR**: [WS/M 17]
**PONTRHYDYRUN** (Croesycielog):
chapel yard [WS/M 19]
**PONTYPOOL** (Old Crane Street):
chapel yard [WS/M 33]
**RISCA** (Bethesda): chapel yard WS/M
17], (Old Moriah): chapel yard
[WS/M 17]
**ST MELLONS** (Caersalem):
[WS/M 40]; [Apply to staff (mfc)]
**SHIRENEWTON** (Gaerllwyd):
[Apply to staff (mfc)]
**TALYWAIN** (Pisgah): chapel yard
[WS/M 33]
**TROSNANT, UPPER** (Pontypool):
chapel yard [WS/M 19]

## MONTGOMERYSHIRE
Monumental Inscriptions
**CARNO**: [WS/M.53]
**LLANDINAM** (Beulah): [WS/M 43]
**LLANFAIR CAEREINION**
(Old burial ground & Zion ): [WS/M 37]
**LLANIDLOES** (Newchapel ):
[WS/M 44]
**LLANLLUGAN** (Caersalem): [WS/M
44]
**MOCHDRE** (Pentre): [WS/M 37]
**SARN**: [WS/M 37]
**WELSHPOOL**: [WS/M 51]

## PEMBROKESHIRE
Monumental Inscriptions
**GELLY**: [WS/M 35]
**LLANDDEWI VELFREY** (Ffynnon):
[WS/M 35
**LLANDISSILIO** (Blaenconin):
[WS/M 35]

## RADNORSHIRE
Registers
**LLANANNO** (Maesyrhelem):
Z 1792-1837 [WS/R 37]
Monumental Inscriptions
**CEFN PAWL**: chapel yard [WS/M 25]
**CWRTNEWYDD** (Llanwenog, Seion):
chapel [WS/M 48]

## OVERSEAS

## AFRICA
Monumental Inscriptions
**KARIEGA** (South Africa): [AFR/M 9]
**THYLO** (Nyasa Mission): [AFR/M 11]

## AUSTRALIA
## NEW SOUTH WALES
Monumental Inscriptions
**ARMIDALE**: [AUA/NSW/M 11]
**PARRAMATTA**: [AUA/NSW/M 10]
**TAMWORTH**: [AUA/NSW/M 13]

## CANADA
## QUEBEC
Registers
**QUEBEC**: Baptist societies: CMB
1860-82 [Mf 1615]; (Sutton Township,
Olivet Baptist): CMB(I) 1850-99
[CAN/QB/R 5]

## INDIA
Registers
**CALCUTTA** (Lall Bazar): C 1800-1908
[IND/L 19]
Monumental Inscriptions
**DACCA**: in chapel [IND/M 37 pp. 46,
136]; (Wari, Old Baptist cemetery)
[IND/M 37 pp. 47]

## USA
## NEW JERSEY
Monumental Inscriptions
**PISCATAWAY** (Samptown Baptist
cemetery): [US/NJ/L 5]
**PISCATAWAY**: History of the Baptist
Churches [includes biographies of
ministers] [US/NJ/L 3]
**PISCATAWAY** (Stelton Baptist
cemetery): [US/NJ/L 3]

## NEW YORK
General
**MIDDLETOWN**: C 1712-87 D 1732-
1811: in Historical & genealogical
miscellany: data relating to the
settlement & settlers of New York &
New Jersey, vol. 2 [US/NY/G 12]
Registers
**MIDDLETOWN**: C 1712-87 D
1732-1811 [US/NY/G 12]
Monumental Inscriptions
**COVERT,** Seneca County:
[US/NY/M 6]
**HECTOR,** Schuyler County (Burdett
Baptist or Tug Hollow Road cemetery):
[US/NY/M 6]

**PENNSYLVANIA**
Registers
**PHILADELPHIA** (First): M 1761-1803
[US/PA/R 2]

**WEST INDIES**
**JAMAICA**
Monumental Inscriptions
**FALMOUTH** (Trelawney) [WI/M 9]
**MONTEGO BAY**: burial ground
[WI/M 9]

# APPENDIX 3

## A LIST OF THE ENGLISH BAPTIST CHURCH RECORDS
## IN THE CUSTODY OF THE
## GOSPEL STANDARD BAPTIST LIBRARY
## 5 HOVE PARK GARDENS,
## HOVE, EAST SUSSEX BN3 6HN

Abbreviations: (P)=Photocopy; (Ts)=Transcript

NOTE: The W numbers in square brackets relate to the number allocated to the church in Whitley, W T, *The Baptists of London* (London 1928)

**BERKSHIRE**

| | | |
|---|---|---|
| FARINGDON | Church Book | 1872-91 |

**CAMBRIDGESHIRE**

GODMANCHESTER see **HUNTINGDONSHIRE**

| | | |
|---|---|---|
| KIRTLING | Church Book | |
| | List of Members[1] | 1893-1904 |

**ESSEX**

| | | |
|---|---|---|
| BURNHAM-ON-CROUCH | Church Book | 1861-1905 |
| WITHAM | Church Book | 1830-41 |
| | Church Book | 1884-1975 |
| | Register of Members | 1884 |

**GLOUCESTERSHIRE**

| | | |
|---|---|---|
| TETBURY | Church Book | 1858-1909 |

---

1. *Now deposited with County Record Office, Shire Hall, Cambridge, CB3 OAP.*

# HAMPSHIRE

**BARTLEY**
| | | |
|---|---|---|
| Hope Chapel, Totton Road | Church Book | 1872-1960 |

**LONGPARISH** | Church Book | 1818-1914 |

# HERTFORDSHIRE

**HERTFORD**
| | | |
|---|---|---|
| Ebenezer Chapel | Church Books[2] | 1773-1928 |

# HUNTINGDONSHIRE

**GODMANCHESTER**
| | | |
|---|---|---|
| | Register of Births[3] | 1801-36 |
| | Church Books[3] | 1825-1947 |

# KENT

**CANTERBURY**
| | | |
|---|---|---|
| Zoar Chapel, Burgate Lane | Church Books | 1843-1913 |

**RAINHAM**
| | | |
|---|---|---|
| Providence Chapel, Orchard Street | Church Book | 1895-1914 |

**TENTERDEN**
| | | |
|---|---|---|
| Jireh Chapel | Church Books | 1844-1950 |

# LANCASHIRE

**BOLTON**
| | | |
|---|---|---|
| Dorset Street, formerly King Street | Church Books | 1876-1956 |

---

2. *Now deposited with County Record Office, Hertford SG13 8DE.*
3. *Now deposited with County Record Office, Grammar School Walk, Huntingdon, Cambs PE18 6LF.*

# LEICESTERSHIRE

| | | |
|---|---|---|
| DESFORD | Church Book | 1795-1809 |

OAKHAM: see **RUTLANDSHIRE**

# LONDON

CHELSEA

| | | |
|---|---|---|
| Grove Chapel [W192] | Church Book | 1850-99 |
| Drayton Gardens, West Brompton, SW10 | Church Books | 1914-43 |

FOREST HILL

| | | |
|---|---|---|
| Zion Chapel [W576] Malham Road, SE23 | Church Book | 1907-63 |

HAMPSTEAD

| | | |
|---|---|---|
| Ebenezer Chapel [W133] Christchurch Passage, New End, NW3 | Church Books | 1825-1957 |

WHITECHAPEL

| | | |
|---|---|---|
| Zoar Chapel [W92] | Church Records | from 1808 |
| Great Alie Street, E1 | Church Book | 1845-79 |
| | Church Book | 1881-1970 |

# OXFORDSHIRE

FARINGDON: see **BERKSHIRE**

# RUTLANDSHIRE

OAKHAM

| | | |
|---|---|---|
| Providence Chapel, | Church Book | 1843-93 |
| New Street | Church Book | 1895-1954 |

## SUFFOLK

**LOWESTOFT**

| | | |
|---|---|---|
| Tonning Street | Church Book | 1868-1916 |

## SURREY

**DORKING**

| | | |
|---|---|---|
| Holmwood Chapel | Church Book (Ts) | 1885-1906 |
| | Church Book | 1907-36 |

**LINGFIELD**

| | | |
|---|---|---|
| Salem Chapel | Church Book | 1925-75 |

## SUSSEX

| | | |
|---|---|---|
| PELL GREEN | Church Book[4] | 1820-44 |
| SHOVERS GREEN | Church Books[4] | 1816-61 |
| | Church Book[4] | 1865-1977 |

## WILTSHIRE

| | | |
|---|---|---|
| AVEBURY | Church Book (P)[5] | 1830-73 |
| | Church Book (P)[5] | 1892-1928 |
| CORSHAM | Church Book (P)[5] | 1858-1977 |
| LUDGERSHALL | Church Book (P)[5] | 1818-19 |
| MARKET LAVINGTON | Church Book (P)[5] | 1832-1932 |
| UPAVON | Church Books (P)[5] | 1858-1978 |

---

4. *Now deposited with East Sussex County Archivist, The Maltings, Castle Precincts, Lewes, East Sussex BN7 1YT.*
5. *The originals of these registers are now deposited with Wiltshire County Record Office, County Hall, Trowbridge, Wiltshire BA14 8JG.*

# APPENDIX 4

## A LIST OF THE ENGLISH BAPTIST CHURCH RECORDS IN THE CUSTODY OF THE STRICT BAPTIST HISTORICAL SOCIETY'S LIBRARY, DUNSTABLE BAPTIST CHAPEL, ST MARY'S GATE, DUNSTABLE, BEDFORDSHIRE LU6 3SW

Abbreviations: (P) = Photocopy; (Ts) = Transcript
NOTE: The W numbers in square brackets relate to the number allocated to the church in Whitley, W T, *The Baptists of London* (London 1928)

**BEDFORDSHIRE**

CARLTON

| | | |
|---|---|---|
| Church Minutes including Lists of Members | 1691-1856 |
| Church Minutes including Lists of Members | 1838-1979 |
| Register of Grown persons and Children | 1788-1833 |

RISLEY (now RISELEY)          Church Minutes          1839-1952

SHARNBROOK
  Bethlehem Chapel          Church Minutes          1833-1904

STOTFOLD
  Rehoboth          Minute Book          1880-1984

**BERKSHIRE**

MAIDENHEAD
  Providence Chapel          Church Minutes          1863-1913

**BUCKINGHAMSHIRE**

ASKETT          Church Minutes          1914-1940

ICKFORD          Church Book (P)          1825-1869

| IVINGHOE | Register of Births | 1793-1837 |
| | Record of Baptisms | 1804-1813 |
| | Church Book (P) | 1804-1973 |
| | (including Births | 1793-1817 |
| | and burials) | 1890-1891 |
| | Church Minutes | 1975-1981 |
| | | |
| LONG CRENDON | Church Book (P) | 1845-1857 |
| | Membership Lists (P) | 1845-1861 |
| | | |
| PENN | Church Books | 1828-1929 |
| | Membership Lists | 1802-1893 |
| | Membership Lists | 1900-1925 |
| | | |
| WADDESDON HILL | Church Book | 1794-1836 |
| | Church Book | 1846-1974 |
| | Register of Burials | 1851-1974 |
| | | |
| WINSLOW | Church Book | 1807-1853 |
| | Register of Births | 1818-1836 |
| | Register of Deaths | 1856-1892 |
| | | |
| WOOBURN GREEN | Church Minutes | c. 1849-1863 |
| | Church Minutes | 1887-1916 |
| | Standing Minutes | c. 1919-1939 |
| | Church Minutes | 1939-1943 |
| | Church Minutes | 1966-1979 |

**CAMBRIDGESHIRE**

| BENWICK | Church Book | 1858- |
| | Church Minutes | 1908-1911 |
| | Church Minutes | 1923 |
| | Church Minutes | 1937-1963 |
| | Marriages | 1930, 1934, 194€ |
| | List of Deaths | 1860-1959 |

CAMBRIDGE
Tenison Road

| | | |
|---|---|---|
| Church Minutes | | 1897-1976 |
| Membership Roll | | 1897-1955 |

COTTENHAM
Ebenezer Chapel,
Rooks Lane

| | |
|---|---|
| Church Minutes | 1819-1979 |
| Membership Lists | 1861-1979 |
| Register of Births | 1800-1844 |

ELSWORTH

| | |
|---|---|
| Church Minutes | 1887-1953 |

STAPLEFORD
Providence Chapel

| | |
|---|---|
| Church Book | 1851-1866 |
| Church Book | 1877-1926 |
| Membership Roll | 1877-1897 |

WILLINGHAM
First Church

| | |
|---|---|
| Church Book | 1726- |
| Church Minutes | 1835-1926 |
| Register of Births | 1792-1833 |
| Births | 1790-1820 |
| Baptisms | 1754-1826 |
| Marriages | 1842-1859 |
| Membership Lists | 1749-1937 |

**CHESHIRE**

LYMM
Cherry Lane

| | |
|---|---|
| Church Minutes | 1893-1942 |
| Church Minutes | 1964-1980 |
| Church Minutes | 1980-1994 |
| Church Register | 1888-1961 |
| and Minutes | 1947-1964 |
| List of 'Named Children' | 1815-1855 |
| Articles, Rules and List of Members | 1980-1992 |

# DEVONSHIRE

### NEWTON ABBOT
| | | |
|---|---|---|
| Old Baptist Chapel | Church Book | 1819-1871 |
| East Street | Church Book | 1874-1919 |

# ESSEX

| EAST MERSEA | Church Minutes | 1804-1902 |
|---|---|---|

### HARWICH
| | | |
|---|---|---|
| Ebenezer Chapel | Church Minutes | 1821-1944 |
| King's Head Street | | |
| (originally Hart Street) | | |

### SAFFRON WALDEN
| | | |
|---|---|---|
| London Road | Church Minutes | 1820-1938 |
| | Membership Roll | 1820-1937 |

# GLOUCESTERSHIRE

### CIRENCESTER
| | | |
|---|---|---|
| Park Street | Church Minutes | 1879-1915 |
| | Membership List | 1840-1908 |

### CUBBERLEY (now COBERLEY)
| | | |
|---|---|---|
| | Church Minutes | 1835-1930 |
| | Membership Roll | 1827-1918 |

### MARSHFIELD
| | | |
|---|---|---|
| Ebenezer Chapel | Church Minutes | 1854-1920 |
| | Membership List | 1854-1908 |

# HERTFORDSHIRE

### HERTFORD
| | | |
|---|---|---|
| Port Vale Independent | Church Book (P) | 1835-67 |
| Calvinistic Chapel | | |

HITCHIN
Bethel Chapel              Church Book (P)                c. 1850-61

HITCHIN
Providence Chapel          Church Minutes                1858-1892
                           Membership List              1858-1890

LONG MARSTON               Church Book (P)               1862-1953
                           Church Book (P)               1955-1971
                           Membership Roll, revised (P)  1932

**HUNTINGDONSHIRE**

HAIL WESTON                Church Book                   1757-1866
                           Church Book                   1869-1901

ST. NEOTS
New Lane                   Register of Births            1808-1842
                           Register of Burials           1853-1896

**KENT**

BETHERSDEN
Union Chapel               Church Book (Ts)              1809-1915
                           Births (Ts)                   1799-1836

BROADSTAIRS
Providence Chapel          Church Minutes                1878-1941
62a High Street

EGERTON                    Church Books (Ts)             1836-1915
                           Membership List (Ts)          1836-1971
                           Register of Burials (Ts)      1863-1984

FARNBOROUGH
Beulah                     Church Minutes                1846-1907
Wellbrook Road [W203]      list of members               1846-1897

| | | |
|---|---|---|
| HADLOW | Church Minutes | 1831-1855 |
| | Church Minutes | 1858-1923 |
| | Church Minutes | 1956-1975 |
| | | |
| MAIDSTONE | | |
| Providence Chapel, | Church Book | 1852-1943 |
| Mote Road | | |
| | | |
| SMARDEN | | |
| Tilden Chapel | Register of Marriges (Ts) | 1840-1984 |
| | Register of Burials (Ts) | 1837-1984 |
| | | |
| TENTERDEN | | |
| Jireh Chapel | Register of Burials (Ts) | 1870-1983 |

**LANCASHIRE**

| | | |
|---|---|---|
| ACCRINGTON | | |
| Zion Chapel, | Church Minutes (Ts) | 1867-1884 |
| Blackburn Road | Church Minutes | 1888-1926 |
| | Membership List | 1867-1888 |
| | | |
| BLACKPOOL | | |
| Reads Avenue | Church Minutes | 1921-1972 |
| (Previously Reads Road) | and list of members | 1921-1979 |
| | Church Minutes and | |
| | List of Members } | 1981-1997 |
| | | |
| BURY | | |
| Providence, Freetown | Church Minutes | 1835-1846 |
| | and List of Members | 1857-1902 |
| | and List of Marriages | 1890-1944 |
| | Church Minutes | 1881-1907 |
| | Church Minutes | 1962-1989 |

| PRESTON | | |
|---|---|---|
| Zoar Chapel | Church Minutes | 1852-1879 |

| ROSSENDALE | | |
|---|---|---|
| Ring's Row, Crawshawbooth | Church Book | 1827-1853 |

| SABDEN | | |
|---|---|---|
| | Church Book | 1835-1843 |
| | Membership List | 1835-1849 |

| STREETGATE | | |
|---|---|---|
| 'Zion's Hill', | Church Book | 1852-1882 |
| Little Hulton | Church Minutes | 1879-1880 |
| Bolton | Membership List | 1852-1882 |

## LINCOLNSHIRE

| BILLINGBOROUGH | | |
|---|---|---|
| High Bridge Street | Church Minutes | 1867-1890 |

## LONDON

| ACTON | | |
|---|---|---|
| Tabernacle [W609] Acton Lane, W3 | Church Minutes | 1881-1971 |

| BETHNAL GREEN | | |
|---|---|---|
| Shalom Chapel [W307], 'Oval', Hackney Road, E2 | Church Minutes | 1889-1908 |

| BRENTFORD | Church Book (P) | 1853-1876 |
|---|---|---|

| DEPTFORD | | |
|---|---|---|
| Zion Chapel [W177], | Church Book | 1842-1881 |
| New Cross Road, SE14 | Membership List | 1887-1890 |
| (originally in | Deacons' Minute Books | 1875-1941 |
| Giffin Street) | Deacons' Minute Books | 1949-1958 |

## FULHAM
Ebenezer Chapel [W693]        Church Book                1913-1972
Lillie Road, SW 6             Register of Members     1889-1940

## ISLINGTON
Zoar Chapel [W258],        Church Minutes         1899-1958
Holloway, Tollington
Park, N4

## ISLINGTON
Ebenezer Chapel [W391],    Church Minutes         1875-1898
Upper Holloway,             Church Minutes         1902-1920
Elthorne Road,              Church Minutes         1935-1946
Hornsey Rise, N19           Membership List       1905-1940

## LEWISHAM
Ladywell [W832],            Church Book             1910-1911
Whitburn Hall,
Whitburn Road, SE13

WALTHAMSTOW   The following are split according to what is written on the book and so may be linked to more than one church building site:

Goodmans Fields [W3]      Church Book and List of Members 1676-1711
                                Church Minutes        1725-1752
                                and List of Members at
                                Wapping [W 48]      1738-1739
                                Church Book           1750-1770
                                  Church Minutes        1752-1783
                                  Register of Members     1833-1935

## WALTHAMSTOW
Little Prescot Street [W3]    Church Minutes         1784-1832
                                  Church Minutes        1832-1844
                                  Church Minutes        1845-1864
                                  Church Minutes        1846-1856
                                  List of Members        1745-1767

## WALTHAMSTOW

| | | |
|---|---|---|
| Commercial Street [W3] | Church Minutes | 1864-1888 |
| | Church Minutes | 1888-1921 |
| | Church Minutes | 1921-1951 |
| | Deacons' Minutes | 1856-1870 |
| | Elders' Minutes | 1891-1904 |
| Membership Transfer Application Book | | 1891-1898 |

## WALTHAMSTOW

| | | |
|---|---|---|
| Zion, Maynard Road [W521] | Church Minutes | 1890-1905 |
| | Church Minutes | 1905-1910 |
| | Membership Roll | 1874-1913 |
| Includes Lord's Day Attendance | | 1905-1913 |

## WALTHAMSTOW

| | | |
|---|---|---|
| Church Hill [W3] | Deacons' Minutes | 1950-1967 |

## WESTMINSTER

| | | |
|---|---|---|
| Pimlico [W129], Carmel Chapel, Westbourne Street, SW1 | Church Minutes | 1839-56 |

## WOOLWICH

| | | |
|---|---|---|
| Enon, High Street [W57] | Church Minutes with Lists of Members | 1754-1806 |
| | Church Minutes with | 1807-1831 |
| | Lists of Members | 1775-1814 |
| | Church Minutes with | 1832-1852 |
| | Lists of Members (with Baptism dates) | 1777-1851 |
| | Church Minutes with | 1852-1884 |
| | Lists of Members | 1802-1856 |
| | Church Minutes with | 1885-1937 |
| | Lists of Members | 1837-1937 |

# MIDDLESEX

BRENTFORD see **LONDON**

## NORFOLK

| GREAT ELLINGHAM | Church Roll (P) | 1701-1789 |

NORWICH
| Orford Hill | Church Minutes | 1857-1975 |
| | Membership Roll | 1858-1911 |

| SHELFANGER | Church Books | 1758-1825 |
| | Church Books | 1834-1940 |
| | Membership Lists | 1765-1825 |
| | Membership Lists | 1834-1877 |
| | Membership Lists | 1880-1920 |
| | Register of Births | 1758-1824 |
| | Marriages | 1904-1920 |

## NORTHAMPTONSHIRE

NORTHAMPTON
| Providence Chapel, | Church Minutes | 1835-1984 |
| Abington Street. | Membership Lists | 1810-1968 |
| Removed to | | |
| the Headlands, 1957 | | |

OUNDLE
| Zion Chapel, | Church Minutes | 1846-1895 |
| Chapel End | Membership List | 1800-1895 |

## NOTTINGHAMSHIRE

SUTTON-IN-ASHFIELD
| Walstone Lane Chapel | Church Book (Ts) | 1770-1865 |

## SUFFOLK

BUNGAY
| Bethesda Chapel, | Church Books | 1852-1960 |
| Chaucer Street | Membership List | c.1846-1939 |

BURY ST EDMUNDS
Rehoboth Chapel,          Church Minutes              1895-1896
Westgate Street

FRISTON                   Church Minutes              1879-1906

GLEMSFORD
Providence Chapel,        Church Minutes              1859-1911
Hunts Hill

SUDBURY
Ebenezer, New Street      Church Minutes (P)          n.d.

**SURREY**

CHOBHAM
West End                  Church Book                 1798-1806
                          Church Book                 1847-1856
                          Church Book                 1858-1886

CROYDON
Derby Road [W540]         Church Minutes              1875-1900
                          Church Minutes              1901-1970
                          Church Minutes              1970-1981
                          Deacons' Minutes            1920-1979
                          Membership Registers        1892-1974

HORLEY
Providence Chapel,        Church Minutes              1846-1945
Lee Street (1846-92)      Membership List             1846-1892
Victoria Road (1892)      Church Minutes              1970-1983

KINGSTON-UPON-THAMES
Zion Chapel [W292],       Church Book                 1922-59
Norbiton, London Road

**SUSSEX**

EAST GRINSTEAD
  Providence                   Church Book                    1890-1952

HORSHAM
  Rehoboth, New Street         Church Minutes and             1834-1836
                               Church Minutes
                               (opposite end of book)         1852-1913
                               Church Minutes                 1913-1942
                               Church Minutes                 1943-1980
                               Burials Book                   1844-1967

WILLINGDON                     Church Minutes                 1938-1967

**WILTSHIRE**

HILMARTON
  Zoar Chapel                  Church Minutes including
                               list of Founding Members       1909-1948

NETHERAVON                     Church Minutes (sparse)        1872-1948
                               Membership List                1835-1913
                               Baptismal List                 1834-1871

**YORKSHIRE**

MASBOROUGH                     Church Minutes                 1862-1864
                               Church Minutes                 1874-1983

# APPENDIX 5

## CHURCH RECORDS CONTAINING BIOGRAPHICAL INFORMATION IN THE ANGUS LIBRARY AND ARCHIVE, REGENTS PARK COLLEGE, OXFORD

N.B. Records less than thirty years old are not open to public inspection without the written permission of the churches concerned.

London churches are cross-referred to Whitley, W T, *The Baptists of London* (London 1928). This volume however should be used with caution as it is in need of revision.

Where county boundaries have changed, the churches are listed under the county in which they lay at the date covered by the records concerned, with a cross-reference from the modern county.

## ENGLAND

**BEDFORDSHIRE**

| BEDFORD | Church Book (facsimile) | 1650-1821 |
|---|---|---|
| KEYSOE | Church Minutes | 1790-1901 |

**BERKSHIRE**

| ABINGDON | | |
|---|---|---|
| Ock Street | Church Books and Minutes | 1721-1986 |
| | Church Membership | 1840-1923 |
| | Births & Burials Registers | 1764-1870 |

| READING | | |
|---|---|---|
| King's Road | Church Book (facsimile & transcript) | 1656-1770 |

| WALLINGFORD | | |
|---|---|---|
| Thames Street | Church Books | 1798-1842 |
| | Church Minutes | 1848-1981 |
| | Births & Burials Register | 1794-1861 |

# BUCKINGHAMSHIRE

| | | |
|---|---|---|
| BUCKINGHAM | Church Book | 1842-1870 |
| NEWPORT PAGNELL<br>Particular Baptist Church | Church Book | 1824-1902 |
| OLNEY | Church Minutes (transcript) | 1775-1814 |
| WENDOVER | Church Books<br>Membership Register | 1844-1928<br>1806-1842 |

# CAMBRIDGESHIRE

| | | |
|---|---|---|
| SOHAM | Church Book (transcript) | 1752-1779 |

# CHESHIRE

| | | |
|---|---|---|
| APPLETON<br>Hillcliffe | Church Minutes | 1877-1900 |

# DEVONSHIRE

| | | |
|---|---|---|
| BAMPTON<br>Calvinistic Baptist | Church Books | 1690-1911 |
| PAIGNTON<br>Barnshill Private Chapel | Church Book | 1836-1846 |
| PLYMOUTH<br>George Street | Church Book (transcript) | 1648-1778 |

# DORSETSHIRE

| | | |
|---|---|---|
| IWERNE MINSTER | Church Book & Minutes | 1865-1960 |

## DURHAM

| | | |
|---|---|---|
| HAMSTERLY | Church Book | 1714-1848 |
| HEXHAM | Church Book | 1651-1680 |

## ESSEX

**HARLOW**
| | | |
|---|---|---|
| Foster Street Burial Ground | Burials Register | 1874 |

## GLOUCESTERSHIRE

| | | |
|---|---|---|
| BOURTON ON THE WATER | Church Book | 1719-1920 |
| | Births & Burials Register | 1811-1898 |
| GUITING POWER & NAUNTON (see also NAUNTON) | Church Book & Minutes | 1837-1931 |
| | Membership Register | 1839-1885 |
| NAUNTON (see also GUITING POWER) | Church Books | 1806, 1830-1844 |
| | Births Register | 1817-1835 |
| | Membership Register | 1839-1885 |

## HAMPSHIRE

| | | |
|---|---|---|
| BAUGHURST | Church Books | 1909-1940 |
| BROCKENHURST | Church Minutes | 1903-1986 |
| | Membership Register | 1922-1937 |
| BROUGHTON | Church Books | 1655-1969 |
| | Graveyard Register | 19th C. |

**ROMSEY**
| | | |
|---|---|---|
| Bell Street | Church Minutes | 1807-1971 |

## HERTFORDSHIRE

**HEMEL HEMPSTEAD**
Boxmoor (Carey from 1980)      Church Minutes          1826-1980
                               Church Roll             1900-1972

**HEMEL HEMPSTEAD**
Leverstock Green               Church Minutes          1946-1967
(Carey from 1980)

**HEMEL HEMPSTEAD**
Marlowes (Carey from 1980)     Church Minutes          1780-1969
                               Burials Ground Register 1866-1875
                               Membership Register     1860-1968

## HUNTINGDONSHIRE

FENSTANTON, WARBOYS            Church Book             1643-1788, 1824
& ST IVES

## KENT

BETHERSDEN                     Births Register (transcript)    1799-1836

BRASTED                        Church Minutes          1877-1989
(church closed 1989)           Membership Register     1877-1939
                               Membership Transfer Books   1897-1962

CHATHAM                        Church Books            1841-1943
Zion, Clover Street            Church Minutes          1965-1986
(closed 1992)                  Burials Register (facsimile)    1785-1837
                               Marriages Register      1899-1990
                               Membership Register     1977-1992
                               Membership Transfers    1923-1969

DOVER
Pentside and Queen Street      Church Minutes          1826-1901
Particular

| EYTHORNE | Births Register (transcript) | 1723-1837 |
|---|---|---|

| GILLINGHAM | | |
|---|---|---|
| Green Street | Marriage Index | 1900-1976 |

| HORSMONDEN | | |
|---|---|---|
| Bramble Street | Church Minutes | 1907-1970 |
| | Membership List | 1886-1913 |

| SANDHURST | Church Book | 1761-1851 |
|---|---|---|

| SHOREHAM | | |
|---|---|---|
| (church closed 1982) | Church Minutes | 1897-1951 |

| SMARDEN | | |
|---|---|---|
| Zion General Baptist | Church Minutes | 1705-1908 |
| (and STAPLEHURST) | Births Register | 1735-1836 |

| SMARDEN | | |
|---|---|---|
| Particular Baptist Chuch | Marriages Register (transcript) | 1840-1977 |
| | Burials Register (transcript) | 1837-1984 |

STAPLEHURST see SMARDEN

| TENTERDEN | | |
|---|---|---|
| High Street, Zion | Church Membership Lists | 1900-1918 |

# LANCASHIRE

| ACCRINGTON | | |
|---|---|---|
| Blackburn Road | Church Books and Minutes | 1760-1901 |

| ACCRINGTON | | |
|---|---|---|
| Cannon Street | Deacons and Church Committee Minutes | 1844-1900 |
| | Church Building Committee Minutes | 1872-1884 |
| | Burials Register | 1833-1864 |
| | Graveyard Accounts (incl burials) | 1857-1901 |

| | | |
|---|---|---|
| **BLACKBURN**<br>Montague Street | Church Minutes | 1927-1960 |
| | | |
| **HASLINGDEN**<br>Trinity | Church Minutes | 1843-1852 |
| | Membership and Baptisms<br>Register | 1831-1863 |
| | | |
| **HUNCOAT**<br>Bethel | Church Minutes | 1902-1919 |
| | Births Register (copy) | 1880-1958 |
| | Church Roll | 1861-1958 |
| | | |
| **LIVERPOOL**<br>Pembroke Chapel | Church Minutes | 1838-1931 |
| | | |
| **MANCHESTER**<br>George Street | Church Minutes | 1823-1844 |
| | | |
| **RAMSBOTTOM** | Church Minutes | 1929-1964 |
| | Membership Transfers | 1898-1943 |
| | | |
| **TOTTLEBANK** | Church Book | 1669-1854 |
| | Church Minutes | 1957-1980 |

## LEICESTERSHIRE

| | | |
|---|---|---|
| WYMESWOLD | Church Minutes | 1883-1914,<br>1938-1961 |
| | Church Roll | 1906 |

## LINCOLNSHIRE

| | | |
|---|---|---|
| BURGH & MONKSTHORPE | Church Book | 1692-1815 |
| | Church Minutes | 1843-1911 |
| | Births & Deaths Register | 1745-1825 |
| | | |
| CONINGSBY &<br>TATTERSHALL | Church Minutes | 1654-1728 |

GOSBERTON
General Baptists,              Quarterly Meetings Minutes     1791-1803
New Connexion

MONKSTHORPE see BURGH

SUTTON                       Church Book                   1797-1837

TATTERSHALL see CONINGSBY

**LONDON AND MIDDLESEX**

Bagnio Court see CRIPPLEGATE

BARBICAN
Goswell Street,              Church Minutes             1682-1740
Glasshouse Yard            Membership List           1717
(meeting at Horsleydown    [Minutes 1741-1854 are in
1764-68, Paul's Alley        the BARBICAN Turner's
1768-80), later               Hall volume]
SHOREDITCH Worship Street  Church Minutes             1855-1881
[W19, W14]                 see SHOREDITCH, Worship Street

BARBICAN
Paul's Alley                Church Minutes             1699-1739
(merged with BARBICAN     Church Minutes see         1768-1780
Goswell Street in 1768) [W14]  BARBICAN Goswell Street

BARBICAN
Turner's Hall              Church Minutes             1695-1699
                          [This volume also includes
                          minutes of BARBICAN Goswell
                          Street 1741-1777 and SHOREDITCH
                          Worship Street 1783-1854]

BEDFONT                  Church Minutes             1937-1944

**BERMONDSEY**

| | | |
|---|---|---|
| Drummond Road | Church Minutes | 1865-1925 |
| [W400] | Membership Registers | 1866-1964 |

**BERMONDSEY**

| | | |
|---|---|---|
| Horsleydown | Church Minutes | 1764-1768 |
| | (see BARBICAN, | |
| | Goswell Street) | |

**BERMONDSEY**

| | | |
|---|---|---|
| Ilderton Road [W748] | Church Minutes | 1916-1978 |

**BETHNAL GREEN**

| | | |
|---|---|---|
| Bethnal Green Road | Church Minutes | 1881-1888 |
| | (see SHOREDITCH, | |
| | Worship Street) | |

**BLOOMSBURY LONG ACRE**

| | | |
|---|---|---|
| King Street [W431] | Church Minutes | 1867-1873 |
| | Church Minutes | 1874-1876 |
| | (see LINCOLNS INN FIELDS, | |
| | Little Wild Street) | |

BOARS HEAD YARD see WHITECHAPEL Petticoat Lane

**BOW**

| | | |
|---|---|---|
| Bow Road | Church Book | 1786-1818 |
| (later Old Ford Road) [W73] | | |

BOW STREET see COVENT GARDEN, Hart Street

**BRIXTON**

| | | |
|---|---|---|
| Wynne Road [W529] | Church Minutes | 1895-1936 |
| | Membership Roll | 1895-1903 |

BRIXTON HALL see LAMBETH

BRUNSWICK SQUARE see ST PANCRAS Henrietta Street

CAMBERWELL
Coldharbour Lane [W89a]          Church Book                    1803-1822

CAMBERWELL
Cottage Green                    Church Book                    1967-1985

CAMBERWELL GATE
Authur Street (formerly          Church Minutes                 1832-1950
WALWORTH Horsley Street)
[W128]

CHELSEA
Paradise Walk                    Church Minutes                 1817-1947
(Lower Sloane Street from        Membership Register            1904-1947
1865) [W108]

COVENT GARDEN
Hart Street                      Church Minutes                 1692-1699
(formerly Bow Street) [W33]

CRIPPLEGATE
Curriers' Hall (meeting at       Church Book                    1689-1723
George Yard in Thames Street
1689, Bagnio Yard off Newgate,
c1692-1703) [W8]

DALSTON JUNCTION see HACKNEY

EAGLE STREET see HOLBORN Kingsgate

FETTER LANE see HOLBORN

GLASSHOUSE YARD see BARBICAN Goswell Street

GOSWELL STREET see BARBICAN Goswell Street

GRAFTON STREET see SOHO

## HACKNEY
| | | |
|---|---|---|
| Dalston Junction [W443] | Church Minutes | 1871-1965 |
| | Membership Registers | 1871-1966 |

## HAMMERSMITH
| | | |
|---|---|---|
| Avenue Road (closed 1939) [W291] | Church Minutes | 1914-1939 |

## HAMMERSMITH
| | | |
|---|---|---|
| New Road | Church Minutes | 1868-1895 |

## HANWELL
| | | |
|---|---|---|
| Westminster Road Union Church [W423] | Church Minutes | 1836-1844, 1866-1958 |

HENRIETTA STREET see ST PANCRAS

## HITHER GREEN
| | | |
|---|---|---|
| Theodore Road [W752] | Church Minutes | 1938-1986 |

## HOLBORN
| | | |
|---|---|---|
| Fetter Lane, Elim Chapel [W71] | Church Minutes | 1784-1839 |

## HOLBORN
| | | |
|---|---|---|
| Keppel Street (formerly SOHO Grafton Street) [W43] | Church Books | 1795-1889 |

## HOLBORN
| | | |
|---|---|---|
| Eagle Street, Kingsgate Chapel [W50] | Church Minutes | 1737-1949 |
| | Membership Registers | 1830-1911 |

HOLBORN see also COVENT GARDEN, LINCOLNS INN FIELDS

HORSLEYDOWN see BERMONDSEY

HOUNSLOW
| Providence, New | Church Minutes | 1868-1971 |
| & Broadway [W239] | Membership Registers | 1868-1914 |

KEPPEL STREET see HOLBORN Keppel Street

KING STREET see BLOOMSBURY LONG ACRE

LONG ACRE see BLOOMSBURY LONG ACRE

LAMBETH
| North Brixton Hall, | Church Minutes | 1872-1874 |
| St Anne's Road [W491] | | |

LINCOLN'S INN FIELDS
| Little Wild Street [W40] | Church Minutes | 1699-1876 |

LION STREET see WALWORTH Lion Street

MAZE POND see SOUTHWARK Maze Pond

NEWGATE Bagnio Court see CRIPPLEGATE

NORWOOD, WEST
| Chatsworth Road [W574] | Church Minutes | 1878-1897 |

OLD FORD see BOW

PAUL'S ALLEY see BARBICAN Paul's Alley

PETTICOAT LANE see WHITECHAPEL

POPLAR
| Cotton Street | Church Book and Minutes | 1808-1853 |
| [W101] | | |

POTTERS BAR
| [W82] | Church Books | 1802-1846, |
| | | 1869-1894 |

REGENT'S PARK
Park Square East                    Church Minutes                  1855-1922
[W279]                              Membership Registers            1856-1922

ST PANCRAS
Henrietta Street                    Church Minutes                  1862-1888
(Brunswick Square) [W109]

SHOREDITCH
Worship Street (formerly            Church Minutes see BARBICAN     1783-1854
BARBICAN Goswell Street;            Goswell Street (in the
met at Bethnal Green Road           BARBICAN Turner's Hall Volume)
1882-1888) [W19]                    Church Minutes                  1855-1888
                                    Baptisms Register               1796-1875
                                    Burials Register (copy)         1785-1837

SOHO
Grafton Street, later               Church Minutes                  1766-1795
HOLBORN Keppel Street               Church Minutes see              1795-1889
[W43]                               HOLBORN Keppel Street

SOUTHWARK
Maze Pond (Old Kent Road            Church Books                    1691-1907
from 1877) [W34]                    Membership Register             1830-1906

SOUTHWARK
Tooley Street, Unicorn Yard         Church Minutes                  1719-1820
[W22]

STEPNEY GREEN
Stepney College Church [W157]       Church Book                     1837-1847
                                    (includes Membership Lists
                                    1825-1847)

THAMES STREET George Yard see CRIPPLEGATE

TOOLEY STREET see SOUTHWARK

TOTTENHAM
High Road [W130]                 Church Minutes                    1827-1968

TOTTENHAM
Westerfield Hall (affiliated to   Church Minutes                    1923-1951
Tottenham High Road) [W675]

TWICKENHAM
Avenue Church [W607]             Marriage Register                 1917-1929

UNICORN YARD see SOUTHWARK, Tooley Street

WALWORTH
East Street [W79]                Church Minutes                    1805-1819

WALWORTH
Horsley Street, later            Church Minutes                    1832-1854
CAMBERWELL GATE                  Church Minutes                    1854-1950
Arthur Street [W128]             see CAMBERWELL GATE
                                 Arthur Street

WALWORTH
Lion Street (Walworth Road       Church Minutes                    1805-1970
from 1863) [W91]                 Membership Registers              1805-1964

WHITECHAPEL
Petticoat Lane, Boars Head       Church Minutes                    1766-1789
Yard [W36]

WOOLWICH
Beresford Street Tabernacle      Church Minutes                    1873-1922
[W288]                           Membership Roll                   1902

WORSHIP STREET see SHOREDITCH

## NORFOLK

GREAT YARMOUTH
Particular Baptist Church          Church Minutes              1752-1907

NORWICH
St Mary                           Members List               1840-1860

## NORTHAMPTONSHIRE

OLNEY see under BUCKINGHAMSHIRE

RAUNDS                            Church Book (transcript)    1798-1908

SLAPTON                           Church Book                 1681-1753

## OXFORDSHIRE

ABINGDON see under **BERKSHIRE**

ASCOT-UNDER-WYCHWOOD   Church Minutes              1949-1994
(closed 1994)

BURFORD                           Church Books                1802-1901,
                                                              1930-1989

CHIPPING NORTON                   Church Minutes              1775-1977
                                  Deaths Register and Burial  1806-1940
                                  Certificates
                                  Burials Register            1846-1895
                                  Church Roll                 1842-1938

COTE                              Church Book (copy)          1647-1882
                                  Church Minutes              1882-1972

EYNSHAM                           Church Minutes              1836-1948
                                  Membership Papers           1840-1851

OXFORD
New Road

| | Church Books | 1833-1975 |
| | Membership Registers | 1780-1956 |

SOUTH HINKSEY                  Church Minutes            1914-1954

WALLINGFORD see under **BERKSHIRE**

**SOMERSETSHIRE**

FROME
Badcox Lane                    Membership Lists          1767

HORSINGTON
Trustees Book

| | Church Minutes | 1827 |
| | Membership List | 1814 |

STOGUMBER                      Births Register (copy)    1779-1884

**SUFFOLK**

BILDESTON

| | Church Books | 1737-1775 |
| | Births Register | 1781-1847 |

FELIXSTOWE
Bethesda

| | Church Minutes | 1912-1913 |
| | Church Roll | 1915 |

IPSWICH
Glebe Lane                     Church Minutes            1825-1830

**SUSSEX**

BRIGHTON
Moulsecoomb Way                Church Minutes            1949-1986

LEWES                          Church Minutes            1806-1812

| RYE | Church Minutes | 1767-1917 |
|---|---|---|

| WIVELSFIELD (later Strict Baptist) | Church Book (transcript) | 1763-1817 |
|---|---|---|

**WILTSHIRE**

| BODENHAM (church closed 1987) | Church Minutes | 1893-1987 |
|---|---|---|

PORTON for Church Book 1655-1687 see BROUGHTON in **HAMPSHIRE**

SALISBURY
| Brown Street | Church Minutes (facsimile) | 1766-1782 |
|---|---|---|
| | Subscribers Book | 1789-1824 |

**WORCESTERSHIRE**

| BROMSGROVE | Church Book (facsimile & transcript) | 1672-1711 |
|---|---|---|

| SHIPSTON-ON-STOUR | Church Books | 1851-1974 |
|---|---|---|

| WESTMANCOTE (closed 1991) | Church Books | 1801-1904, 1966-1990 |
|---|---|---|

**YORKSHIRE**

| BIRKBY | Church Minutes | 1879-1882 |
|---|---|---|

# WALES

**EAST GLAMORGAN**

CARDIFF
Longcross                          Church Minutes                          1929-1951

# APPENDIX 6

## A LIST OF LONDON BAPTIST CHURCH RECORDS IN THE CUSTODY OF GUILDHALL, REGENT'S PARK COLLEGE AND DR WILLIAM'S LIBRARIES

*Abbreviations   Guildhall (G), Regents Park College   & Dr Williams's (W)*
*[W] number allocated to the church in Whitley, W.T., The Baptists of London*


**ARTILLERY LANE, Spitalfields [W.5]**

| | |
|---|---|
| Acts 1701-1702 | G 20, 228/1B |
| Minutes 1716-1727 | G 20, 228/1A |

**DEVONSHIRE SQUARE [W.5]**

| | |
|---|---|
| Memoranda etc. 1664-1676, 1690-1702, 1702-1727 | G 20, 228/1A |
| Register of Members 1664-1706 | G 20, 230 |
| Register of Members 1837-1871 | G 20, 231 |
| Register of Members transferred 1883-1887 | G 20, 233 |
| Register of Members received & dismissed 1885-1888 | G 20, 234 |
| Minutes 1727-1750 | G 20, 228/ |
| Minutes 1762-1779 | G 20, 228/4 |
| Minutes 1779-1947 (9 vols) | G 20, 228/5-15 |
| List of Members 1750-1759 | G 20, 228/3 |
| Dissolved & united with Turner's Hall | G 20, 228/B |

**GLASSHOUSE YARD [W.19]**

| | |
|---|---|
| Church Book 1680-1740 | R F.P.C.C.11 |
| Church Book 1741-1832 (transcribed) | |

**PAUL'S ALLEY, Barbican [W.14]**

| | |
|---|---|
| Church Book 1695-1739 (part transcribed) | R A.b.5 |
| Church Book 1739-1768 (transcribed) | W 38.74 |
| List of Members 1739-1763 (transcribed) | W 38.73 |
| Transcriptions of part of the above | G 20, 953 |

**PETTY FRANCE, Westminster [W.5]**

| | |
|---|---|
| Members 1676-1690 | G 20, 228/1B |
| Memoranda of acts 1675-1701 | G 20, 228/1B |
| List of Members 1676-1690 | G 20, 228/1B |

**SHACKLEWELL,** Stoke Newington [W.114]
    Founded 1822,
    United with Devonshire Square 1884
    Archives with Devonshire Square           G 20, 245-9
    Church meetings 1828-1883              G 20, 246
    Register of Members 1822-1841           G 20, 248

**TURNER'S HALL,** Philpot Lane [W.5]
    Minutes and Members 1676-1690          G 20, 228/1B
    Minutes etc. 1716-1727                 G 20, 228/1B

**WALBROOK** [W.5]
    Memoranda and Members 1708-1718        G 20, 228/1B

**WHITES ALLEY,** Moorfields [W.1]
    Minutes Moorfields 1681-1745           G 592
        Paul's Alley, Barbican 1745-1779
        Worship Street (Hog Lane) 1779-1829
        Trinity Place, Borough 1829-1832
        Cole Street, Dover Road 1833-1840
        Stamford Street, Blackfriars Road 1840-1841